Lo...

SKID ROW BEAT

A Street Cop's Walk on the wild Side

Paladin Press • Boulder, Colorado

Also by Loren Christensen:

Anything Goes: Practical Karate for the Streets
Deadly Force Encounters: What Cops Need to Know to
    Mentally and Physically Prepare for and Survive a Gunfight
Far Beyond Defensive Tactics: Advanced Concepts, Techniques,
    Drills, and Tricks for Cops on the Street
Fighting Power: How to Develop Explosive Punches,
    Kicks, Blocks, and Grappling
How to Live Safely in a Dangerous World
Skinhead Street Gangs
Speed Training: How to Develop Your Maximum Speed for Martial Arts
The Way Alone: Your Path to Excellence in the Martial Arts
The Way of the Warrior: The Violent Side

Skid Row Beat: A Street Cop's Walk on the Wild Side
by Loren W. Christensen

Copyright © 1999 by Loren W. Christensen

ISBN 1-58160-012-7
Printed in the United States of America

Published by Paladin Press, a division of
Paladin Enterprises, Inc., P.O. Box 1307,
Boulder, Colorado 80306, USA.
(303) 443-7250

Direct inquiries and/or orders to the above address.

PALADIN, PALADIN PRESS, and the "horse head" design
are trademarks belonging to Paladin Enterprises and
registered in United States Patent and Trademark Office.

CONTENTS

Introduction 1

PART ONE: SEX 7

69 9
The Hand Job 11
No Handicap 13
Rosie 15
Yolanda 17
The Blond Boy 20
Grocery Cart Babe 22
The Naked Dancer 24
The Yellow Bus 27
Pressed Breasts 29
Love in a Dumpster .31
She's Packin' 33

PART TWO: VIOLENCE 35

Fun with Prisoners 37
Whoops! 39
Don't Let Us Disturb Your Game 42

Don't Mind Me, I'm Just Bleeding 44
The Open Window 45
Ernie Bigbear 48
I'll Keep an Eye Out for It 52
A Rose for a Wino 54
Just Sittin' in the Sun 56
Iceman 58
No More Trophies 59
Gypsy: She's a Man Eater 61
When Jimmy Diss'd Chief's 64
Knockin' at Death's Door 66
Right in the Kisser 69
The Wrestler and the Car Door 71
My Glasses 74
The Arsonist 76
Van Gogh 79
Stolen Wallet 81
The Bridge 84
Roll Playing 88
Time for a Vacation 91

PART THREE: BODILY EXCRETIONS **95**

Wine Shits 97
It's All Good 98
A Good Defense 101
White Stuff 102
They're in the Trunk 104
The Brick Shit House 107
Brain Goo 110
Fighting in the John 114
Dissin' My Police Car 116
People Watching 117
A Hat Full of Sunshine 118
Sweet Love 120

CONTENTS

Damn Gravity 122
The Expert Judge 125
View from a Window 127

PART FOUR: CHARACTERS .131

A Do-It-Yourself Job 133
The John Wayne Impersonator 135
Mmm, Mmm Good 137
Shaken Not Stirred 139
Officer Cross 140
Easy Money 143
U.S.S. Monroe 145
John Lee's Hats 146
Got a Light? 148
The Apology 150
Frankenstein 152
Walk, Damn It! 154
Waking Up Drunks 156
Officer Cocky Hat 158
Got a Dollar? 160
The Gypsy and the Cigarettes 162
Officer Sonny's Death 165
Halloween 168
Dog-Eatin' Sue 170
The Businessman 172
Wilbur and His Skivvies 175
The Guy in the Phone Booth 177
The Old Burglar 179
A Flophouse Death 180
Old Mary F 183
The Bottle Is the Deadliest Weapon 184

ACKNOWLEDGMENTS

Police officers love to tell war stories, so it wasn't hard to get skid row veterans to reminisce about their years working that place "Forgotten by God," as one officer put it. Many thanks to them for their anecdotes, some of which were clean enough for me to include in this book.

To my wife, Donna, and my kids, Carrie, Dan, Amy, and Kelly. Thanks for always listening as I read my day's writing to you; I need and appreciate your feedback. Also, thanks for your support for my obsession with writing and your understanding and patience when the stress of those last few days on a book project makes me cranky.

INTRODUCTION

I had a college professor back in the '60s

who enthralled me with tales of his adventures living on the streets of Portland, Oregon's skid row. He hadn't been down and out; he did it to research a paper on what it was like to have to survive without money, food, family, and any of the amenities and luxuries most of us have grown accustomed to. He told of begging for food, sleeping in doorways, and getting pushed around by street people. He did it for two weeks but quit when he got sick from living in the filth.

I was 20 years old when he told me his stories, and I thought the idea was the coolest thing I had ever heard. I knew a little about skid row, since my buddies and I used to drive through it—wide eyed and with our doors locked—on the way to cruise Broadway further uptown. Occasionally we would gather our courage, pull to the curb, and ask a wino to buy us a six-pack of beer. Only once did one return with our brew. All the other times they disappeared with our money, probably laughing at the dumb college boys as they bought themselves a bottle of Mad Dog 20/20, the rotgut of choice on the row.

I loved the professor's stories, because at 20 I had yet to have one adventure, and I was starving for lots of them. I fantasized for a long time about living for two or three weeks on the mean streets of skid row, then writing my adventures in a college term paper. Well, my college year ended without my having a skid row adventure, though I was destined to move on and have many others over the years.

Two years later, I found myself in Vietnam having an adventure I couldn't have imagined back when I was sitting comfortably in that class listening to the prof's stories.

A year after I returned home, I joined the Portland Police Bureau, where one of my first assignments as a rookie was working with a training officer patrolling Portland's rockin' and rollin' 12-square-block skid row. I thought about my professor as we drove into skid row that first night—and how weird fate can be. I worked there only a few months that first time, but 10 years later, after having worked several other assignments, I returned and spent five years patrolling the row in a car and walking a foot beat.

I would guess that most major cities have a skid row, and I would also guess that most of them are in flux—slowly giving way to renovation, modernization, and yuppieization, if you will. Portland's skid row has been in transition for about 12 years and is now called Old Town. Although there are still a few of the old taverns, missions, and flophouses, they are being squeezed out by cute little boutiques, ethnic eateries, and gourmet coffee places. Winos are being replaced by buyers and sellers of drugs, who are beginning to attract street gangs.

Perhaps it's just in the mind of those of us who patrolled those mean streets a few years ago, but there is still a sense of the place that it once was. Every time I pass through the area, I reflect back on my first night of patrol there and a call we had at Third and Couch. I remember how the flashing blue and red lights atop the four idling patrol cars brought color and life to the dreary intersection. I recall how the police lights created a mob of ghostly and distorted shadow people that stretched up the sides of the decaying buildings, draped over rusted cars, and fell across urine-stained sidewalks. The shadow people were twice as large as the real people who were huddling together and shivering in their drab Salvation Army-issue coats against a biting November midnight wind. While the real people stood motionless and stared at the covered body lying in the gutter, the shadow people danced merrily in the pulsating disco light.

2

INTRODUCTION

We were at an intersection smack in the heart of skid row, an area surrounded by flophouses, long-ago abandoned buildings, taverns, used clothing stores, porno shops, and a multitude of stumbling drunks. I can't remember why the guy in the gutter was dead. He might have been murdered; he might have fallen in a drunken haze and cracked his head on the curb; he could have been hit by a car; or maybe he'd just given up the struggle of living.

Death is common on the streets of skid row. Sometimes a man will lie on the sidewalk for several days as business people step over him on their way to their high-rises. Then a walking-beat cop will kick his shoe a couple of times to wake him and discover the man has been long dead. One morning as I was racing to a call, I noticed a guy lying on the sidewalk. I don't know why I zeroed in on him, since there were at least two dozen others sleeping it off along the same stretch. I was busy the rest of the day and never got back to the area. The next day I got a call on a dead body, and sure enough it was the same guy, still lying there after all the others had sobered and left. The medical examiner said he had died of natural causes and had been there for at least three days. Hundreds of people had stepped over or around him, but no one had stopped to see if he was OK.

Skid row people usually die unceremoniously: in a doorway, on a flophouse mattress, in a debris-strewn alleyway. Or they steal a bottle from another wino and get beaten to death for the transgression.

There are criminals of every ilk on skid row: thieves, rapists, dopers, murderers, prostitutes, and every other type of predator watching and waiting for an easy victim. Together they make life on skid row a Wild West show, a place where anything can happen— and usually does.

Cops are strange bedfellows to these people. They are respected, feared, depended upon, avoided, sought after, hated, and sometimes victimized. One minute a cop is strictly enforcing the law, and the next minute he's acting like a loving parent. Some cops love the people there; others see them as less than human. Some feel these conflicting emotions in the same shift.

There are different rules for the inhabitants of skid row and for the cops who spend a third of their lives there. These rules favor some and disfavor others. The district attorney doesn't like different rules; nor do the bleeding-heart social workers. But then they don't live there. They don't have to survive those mean streets every day as do the street people and the cops.

This is a book of stories about things observed and experienced by me and other cops who know skid row, some having spent most of their careers there. The stories paint a vivid picture of the people, events, and the daily routine of a place that few non-skid row people have experienced or understand, since most avoid the place.

Some of the stories are painfully honest, in that they show cops as human beings at their worst. You may not like what they did, but don't judge them too quickly if you haven't walked the same path they have. Of course, this doesn't make it right if their actions were an abuse of power. It shows, however, that behind the symbolic uniform and badge are human beings who are susceptible to failings of spirit and who have a breaking point in a world where only a few can survive for long.

But there are also tales that show cops at their best—as peacemakers, psychologists, mothers, fathers, and loving disciplinarians. They are men and women in a unique position to have touched human lives that are barely hanging onto the lowest rung.

Many of the stories happened more than 25 years ago, others happened while I was writing this book and were told to me by officers who work in skid row today. I have put the stories into four categories—Sex, Bodily Excretions, Violence, and Characters—though many of the tales could fit into more than one. The real names of officers, winos, and other players have been changed and locations renamed because they aren't essential to the stories. Four of the stories were written by Ed Miller, a deceased officer who wrote a column for the Portland Police Association's monthly newspaper, *The Rap Sheet*. Those stories carry his byline.

There is no other place in the world like skid row. My objective in telling these stories is to capture the essence of the human condition that exists in a place that is disappearing into history. You will

INTRODUCTION

no doubt find many of these stories gross, disgusting, funny, sad, mysterious, and offensive. If you are sensitive to political correctness, you won't find it here.

Such is the place called skid row.

PART ONE

SEX

There is a section about sex for two reasons.
One, it helps sell books (bet you opened the book here
first, right?). Two, sex happens on skid row, although
many times it's a little different from sex outside of the
row (then again, maybe not). Those pickled winos who
still know what sex is, and even have a need for it, have a
difficult job at best finding a willing partner. Years of
drinking, falling face first onto the sidewalk, sleeping in
doorways, and having angry fists, clubs, and bottles
smashed into their heads play havoc on people's looks,
thus reducing their attraction to persons of the opposite
sex. Therefore, when the need gets overpowering, they
take what they can get.

And that's when it can get a little weird.

69

About my third day on the job, my coach and I took a guy to jail. Although I had been a military policeman in the army and had dealt with a lot of drunk soldiers, I had never seen a big-city drunk tank. After we booked in our guy, I asked if I could see where the drunks ended up, as I had heard that Portland had tanks that were quite large. My coach nodded and led me back into the dank, dark subculture of gray bars and horrific smells.

A drunk tank, as the name implies, was simply a large cell where 30 to 40 men and women slept off their drunks. They have disappeared in most cities now, since alcoholism is considered a disease, and tanks are inhumane treatment for people with an illness. But they existed in the '70s, and they were horrific places where the inebriates would slump into corners, sprawl out on the urine-wet cement floor, curl up in a fetal position against a wine-shit-stained wall, and often fall into a drunken sleep in the middle of grappling with one another over a cigarette butt.

As we walked down the dark aisle between rows of cells, voices shouted and cursed as hands reached for us through the bars. It was an odd sight, because some of the cells were so dark that the hands seemed dismembered, almost as if they were a life force unto themselves. I was amazed at how much expression could be conveyed in the configuration of fingers and a twist of the wrist. Some hands reached out for help, as if they had awakened to the realization of how low they had sunk. Other reached out with fingers that were claw-like. Some reached out just wanting human contact with people who had not fallen into the same shadowy depths of despair.

A hand grabbed my jacket sleeve and pulled me toward the cell. It startled me, and I reflexively jerked my arm away and stepped into the center of the aisle.

"Yeah," my coach said. "Stay in the center. One time one of my trainees was grabbed by a hand and that was the last I ever saw of the kid."

There was a monstrously overweight black jailer standing at the end of the aisle. "Hey, what's up fellas?" he called as we neared.

"Nothin' much," my coach said. "My pup here just wanted to see the drunk tank. Givin' him a little tour."

The jailer chuckled the way fat men do with their belly. "Then you'll want to check out my two lovebirds here on the floor."

"What you got," my coach asked as we stopped next to the jailer.

The jailer chuckled again. "Couple of winos in love, but too drunk to enjoy it." He pointed with his nightstick toward the cell floor where two old winos were lying on the wet floor, dead asleep. But what separated them from the others was that they were lying on their sides, stomach to stomach, in opposite directions. Both had pushed their soiled pants and skivvies down to their ankles, and both had their faces in the other's crotch. One man's limp penis was pressed against the other man's chin, and the other man's unit was draped across his lover's nose. Their mutual, slobbering snores were like chain saws in a forest.

The big jailer's belly chuckled again. "Looks like they were having a little afternoon delight, but the wine passed 'em out before they could get very far." He shook his head and did his chuckle again. "Guess you can find love anywhere."

THE HAND JOB

I was working with a trainee one night, doing a slow cruise along 9th Avenue, eye-balling all the activity on the teeming sidewalks. Phil had just been hired by my department; however, he had worked five years as a patrol officer in Detroit. He knew how to communicate with people OK, he just had to learn how we did things in Portland. But in a couple of minutes, he was to show me how they did things in Detroit.

We were about a block away from the busiest intersection on skid row when Phil called for me to stop. He was looking out his passenger's window as he told me to back up a few feet. "Keep backing," he said, rolling down his window. "A little more . . . there. Look." He was pointing toward a darkened doorway across the street. "Look at those two guys," he said.

I leaned over and peered out the window in the direction he was pointing. There were two guys sitting on the doorway stoop, a tall, skinny black guy, who I knew as Lamont Washington, and a white guy I had never seen before. Washington was gay and, as usual, was wearing white women's boots, a beige women's overcoat complete with a fake fur collar, shabby slacks, and a tank top. The other guy was sitting close to him, his back propped against the door with his tattered wino pants and underwear bunched around his ankles.

"That black guy is giving the white guy a hand job," Phil laughed.

I thought that was what I was seeing, but my mind wasn't accepting it. I squinted and leaned forward until I was practically lying across Phil's lap. "Damn," I said. "You're right."

Phil reached between the seats and grabbed his six-cell, steel mag flashlight. "Can I show you how we would handle this in Detroit?"

"Sure," I said shrugging. "Have at it. But it looks like the white guy is already getting it handled."

Phil smiled a shit-eating grin and quietly opened the car door, then shut it just as quietly behind him. Like Sylvester the Cat dart-

11

ing from tree to tree in the cartoons, he tiptoed to the back of the car, then over to a burnt out streetlight, then to the rear of a parked car, then quickly across the street, where he flattened himself against a wall about 20 feet to the right of the preoccupied couple in the doorway. I had no idea what he was going to do.

Phil flattened himself even more against the wall, then ninja-like, slowly sidestepped his way toward the sex scene. Since the doorway was slightly inset, the two lovers couldn't see the uniformed cop sneaking up on them. He inched his way along the wall until he was next to the doorway, and then he looked over at me and nodded with a huge smile as he brought his steel flashlight up near his shoulder. On the stoop, Washington's hand was a blur.

I don't remember if Phil did a karate yell as he stepped around the corner, but I remember how fast he brought down that steel light onto the fine bones of Washington's loving hand, a hand that was so lovingly gripping his friend.

In the next second or two, three series of screams came from that doorway. First, the white guy and Washington screamed together because Phil's sudden appearance scared the shit out of them. Then Washington screamed again when the flashlight struck his hand. The third scream came from the white guy, because when that loving hand was struck, Washington reflexively clenched his fingers in a death grip on the man's unit.

Phil bee-lined across the street and jumped into the patrol car. "Come on, move it," he said. "Let's get out of here."

I did just that, stomping the accelerator and laying a little patch of rubber. In the rearview mirror, I could see Washington and his friend hopping up and down in agony, Washington holding his throbbing hand, his friend clutching his throbbing dick.

NO HANDICAP

Officer Crandon is about as conservative as you can get—even for a skid row street cop. He's not a deeply religious man, but he sees situations as either right or wrong, black or white. I've never seen him do anything prejudicial against gays or lesbians, but he definitely believes the life-style is wrong. It's this view that has kept him from getting promoted, even though he scored in the top percentile of the written test and has done an excellent job on the oral—except for the question that pertains to the acceptance of homosexuality as a viable life-style. He refuses to say that it's OK, even though he understands that the police department now accepts all life-styles. He absolutely believes homosexuality is wrong and refuses to prostitute himself and say what the department wants to hear. Because of his conviction, he remains a street officer today, and one of the most honest ones you will ever meet.

"I was a rookie and had been working a few months by myself," Crandon said. "I worked all over downtown, occasionally on skid row. In those days, there was a gay bar called Bruce's, one of many gay places in the area, but it was the absolute worst. It was a disgusting hole, crowded with degenerates who were into everything a sick mind could think of. I had to go in there a couple times on calls, and I absolutely hated it. There was a huge sign over the bar that greeted you like a slap in the face when you walked in: 'LIVE TO BUTT FUCK.' Can you believe that?

"I was cruising by the place one night and noticed a car in the handicap parking zone out front, a little MG car. It was pouring down rain, so I wrote the ticket inside my car, then I dashed over to hang the tag on the MG's windshield. That's when I saw movement inside.

"I looked into the fogged windows and saw a guy behind the wheel looking back at me. Then I saw another guy's head come off the driver's lap. Can you believe that?

"'Is everything all right?' the sucker guy asked me after the window rolled down.

"I didn't know what to do or say. So I said, 'Don't park here anymore. You don't look handicapped.' What else could I say? I was so embarrassed.

"Bruce's closed down after the AIDS epidemic broke out. Now it's a place where runaways and street kids spend the night and get food.

"But I sure was embarrassed about that deal in the MG."

ROSIE

Her name was Rosie, and she was the feistiest, homeliest 60-year-old woman to come out of the dregs of skid row. She looked like a bag lady minus the grocery cart: layers of dresses, tops, jackets, some whole, some in parts. She had a witch-like face, a laugh that cackled, and a voice that would drown out a rock band. Sometimes she was falling-down drunk, and other times she just acted crazy. I'm assuming that she must have been on medicine to control her mood swings, and most of the time she was out of it.

Every officer who worked skid row during the three or four years Rosie was there got calls on her disrupting traffic. There is a busy four-lane street bordering skid row, which intersects with six major streets that pass through the area. Countless times, Rosie would block traffic in one of them and shout profanities in her unique way, which included lifting her dress or dresses, thrusting her hips forward, grabbing her crotch and blaring in that raspy, ragged voice, "Come on boys! I'm sittin' on a million-dollar gold mine here. Gots it right here for you." She would repeat this over and over as she rubbed herself vigorously and crab-walked toward a sharp-looking man, albeit a shocked one, usually sitting behind the wheel of a BMW.

Our 911 got so many calls on Rosie that the dispatchers, though 20 miles away from skid row, knew by the complainant's description that the traffic problem was the infamous Rosie, proclaiming to all that she was sitting on a million-dollar gold mine.

I took her to the detox many times. Sometimes she would go willingly and we would have fun with her on the drive; other times she would fight like a wildcat. One time, I had to wrestle her into the backseat (you never look good fighting with a 60-year-old woman) and she landed hard on her back. Then with the car door open and my hand resting on the door frame, I turned to say something to my partner. I was distracted only a moment, but that's all it took for Rosie to smash the hard heel of her shoe into my thumb. I have nearly a one-inch scar there to remind me of my screw-up.

15

Today, the detoxification center in Portland is somewhat like a hospital—clean, polished, with lots of regulations to ensure that the occupants are treated humanely. The first detox, however, consisted of a large room, separated into six-by-six-foot cubicles with walls of chicken wire (thin, interwoven wire with one- to two-inch-wide octagon-shaped spaces).

Rosie found herself in one of those chicken-wire rooms at least once or twice a week. We noticed that she was always popular with other winos, but we didn't know why, though in our police-trained minds we had our suspicions. Then one day we found out for sure.

Officer Davidson had just deposited a falling-down drunk into a cage and was on his way out of the smelly place when he saw a commotion on the far side of the room. Since he couldn't make out what was happening by looking through the many walls of wire, he worked his way along the maze of walkways, sidestepping puddles of urine and vomit that had run out from the cages. Just as he turned down the last walkway, he stopped dead in his tracks; his eyes widened to the size of dinner plates.

The cages were not coed, nonetheless Rosie hadn't let that slow her down. If she noticed Davidson walk up, she didn't let on; nor did her friendly neighbor who occupied the next cage. Rosie was bent over at her waist, hands resting on her knees, with her butt pressed up against the chicken wire wall. Her neighbor, who Davidson says had to be named Longfellow, was pressed against the other side of the chicken wire that had all those octagon holes.

Both were having the most fun they could have without laughing.

YOLANDA

His name was Yolanda, at least that's the name he assumed after he started taking female hormone shots. He was an odd-looking thing, albeit somewhat attractive: a mix of male and female, Caucasian and Hispanic, with broad, masculine shoulders and heavy cheek rouge. He was fairly articulate and used feminine gestures with soft hands that fluttered about in the air like butterflies. He always dressed neutrally, like "Pat" in the old Saturday Night Live shows, generally wearing a tight, soiled T-shirt that revealed a square, male chest, but with two bumps where breasts had formed. Toward the end of the month when Yolanda had drunk away all of his state checks and had no money for his hormone shots, his breasts would begin to shrink and his facial whiskers would start poking through his makeup.

He was always polite to me when he was sober, but he could get a little cantankerous when he was drunk. Once when he got hurt in a fight, I had to call for an ambulance, which he didn't like, though he was hurt quite badly. He fought the medics and me as we strapped him into the gurney and shoved him into the rear of the ambulance. That was the first time I had been in a closed-in space with him, and I recall that his body odor was beyond horrible, probably sweat accumulation from dozens of wino lovers.

And there were always lots of winos around him. I assumed that many didn't know he was a he, while the others were too horny to care—or admit it to themselves. He was always hanging on a different guy, sometimes several. My guess is that he was happily promiscuous and that those with him were happy that he was that way.

My partner Karen and I had several contacts with him, and for some reason she was more disgusted with Yolanda's odd sexuality than I was. I always teased her that she was offended because Yolanda was so much more feminine than she.

There is a bank lot on the edge of skid row where on Sundays Karen and I used to park and write our reports. From the upper parking lot, we could look down on a small park at the corner of an

17

intersection where traffic was practically nonexistent on weekends. Winos gathered in the little greenery, usually sitting on a long bench and drinking from brown paper bags. Occasionally when we cruised by we would stop and break up a fight and pour out the contents of their bottles. Most of the time, we just left them alone since they were away from the core area of the city.

One day, Karen and I were on the upper lot eating our lunch. Below us in the park were a half dozen winos perched on the bench swapping slugs from a big jug, oblivious to the fact that we were above them on the other side of a guardrail. We had no intentions of doing anything about it anyway, especially since we were eating our lunch. We looked down at them occasionally, but mostly concentrated on our lunch and gossip.

Then Yolanda walked up to the bench.

"Hey, it's Yolanda," Karen muttered around a big bite of a sandwich.

I purposely raised my eyebrow and shot her a look. "Gee, you sound almost excited."

"Oh sure," she said, shaking her head. "Actually, he'd be more interested in you than in me."

We continued eating and chatting, while watching Yolanda and the boys. He stood before the bench and talked to them as if holding court, laughing and moving about like a giddy cheerleader with nervous energy. Then after a few minutes, he began looking right and left, as if checking to see if anyone was watching.

"What the hell is he doing?" Karen sputtered, nearly choking on a cookie.

Yolanda had kneeled down between the knees of the first guy on the end of the bench, who we could see was doing something to his pants. Then her head disappeared, then reappeared, then disappeared, then . . .

"Oh my God," Karen gasped. "It looks like Yolanda is—"

For some reason it struck me funny. "Looks like he's having lunch."

A moment later, Yolanda looked up at the wino and smiled, then sidestepped on her knees to the next guy, where again his head disappeared between a pair of knees. Astonished, Karen and I watched silently through the windshield. Three minutes later, Yolanda sidestepped to the next guy. Above them, we continued to watch. And watch some more.

"Karen?" I said a few minutes later. My voice sounded loud in the car, though it couldn't have been more than a whisper. I continued to look out the window.

"What?" Her eyes stayed focused on the action.

"This is really sick." A few seconds passed before we slowly turned and looked at each other. We burst into laughter.

"Let's get out of here," she said, stuffing her napkin into her lunch bag.

"You want to go down there and break that up?" I asked, looking over my shoulder as I backed up.

"Nah," Karen said. "They're having more fun than us. Let's leave them alone."

THE BLOND BOY

I worked juveniles for three years, a job that I loved and hated simultaneously. The part I hated was having to go into the schools and give presentations to students in 7th and 8th grade. At that age, the kids are obnoxious at best and really, really obnoxious at worst. But the second part of my job, investigating child abuse, I found rewarding. I felt as if I were making a difference when I got a kid out of an abusive situation.

We worked side by side with Children's Services Division (CSD) and got to know some of the CSD workers quite well. One woman, Maria Giani, a 40-something single mother of one, was a particular joy to work with. She had remained enthusiastic about her job over the years, even with all the frustrations and heartache that come with working in a system that chews up and spits out even the best of people. She loved kids and worked hard to get them help when life had dealt them a shitty hand, such as a drunken and abusive father, doped-up neglectful mother, or lecherous grandfather. For several days, the sergeant had been telling us at roll call of phone calls the secretaries had been getting about a little blond-haired boy seen hanging around skid row. The callers all agreed that he looked to be about eight or nine, cute as a button, with a mop of blond hair. He was usually seen in a group of winos on a corner or walking with one or two on a back street.

It wasn't unusual to see kids on skid row, but normally they were with a family who had come into bad luck. For sure they were in a terrible place, but at least they were with their parents. The blond boy, the callers said, seemed to be with no one. The sergeant told us to drive through skid row whenever we got a chance to look for him. Two days later I saw him.

He was standing on the corner amongst a group of drunks who were tousling his hair and rubbing his little shoulders. I anchored my car and leaped out into the midst of the winos. I grabbed the boy by his arm, but because I was wearing civilian clothes the winos got vocal and threatened to stick a knife in me. It was clear that they didn't like the idea I was taking their boytoy. When two of them moved toward me, I pulled my weapon and encouraged them to continue coming so I could dump my 9mm rounds into their chests. I knew what they had been doing to the boy, and I was pissed. They got the message and backed off.

Back at the office, the boy refused at first to give me his name or say what had been going on. After an hour, though, he began to lose his tough exterior. He told me that he had run away, and for the past week he had been "sucking on those men's things" to earn food and drink. I wished then that I had shot the bastards.

He said his first name was Tony—Tony Giani—and that his mother worked for CSD. Now I remembered seeing his picture proudly displayed in Maria's office cubicle.

Their reunion was heartwarming, but as a mother she could sense that everything wasn't right with her son, that something had happened in the long week he had been gone. I got one of the other CSD workers to take the boy into the break room to get him a soda, then I told Maria what her son had been forced to do.

I'm not sure how I would have reacted, but she took the news with quiet stoicism, though there was pain in her eyes. Lots of it. She thanked me and I left.

We never made an arrest in the case because the mother wanted to quickly get her son on the path of healing. I left juveniles a few months later and returned to working patrol. I never saw the mother or the boy again, though about four years later I got a letter from her. She said that Tony had healed from the experience and was maturing into a typical teenager. He was getting As and Bs in school and was doing marvelously. She thanked me for my part and said she was still working for CSD.

GROCERY CART BABE

Tammi was four feet tall, if that; I don't know if that made her a midget or a dwarf. It was hard to tell how tall she was because I can only recall a few times seeing her walk on her own accord. Usually she rode around on the back of her boyfriend-of-the-day, or she would ride in a grocery cart like a toddler at the super market.

I would see her all over town being pushed in that cart, usually sharing the ride with a couple of sleeping bags, clothing, and 50 soda bottles that had been collected to turn in for a nickel refund each. Sometimes the cart would be over-jammed with stuff, and I would assume she was moving to a new flophouse or under a freeway overpass, especially if it was the middle of the month and she was between welfare checks.

For the past six months, she'd had the same boyfriend, an unusual thing on skid row. He was tall, not bad looking, but drank to excess, which often affected his driving ability—driving the grocery cart, that is. The couple generally behaved themselves, and I don't remember taking them to jail, though I did run them to the detox center a few dozen times. I took a big club out of their cart once, just because they were drunk and hanging on a corner with a bunch of other drunks.

She wasn't a bad looking lady and was amply blessed in the chest area. I didn't know if it was because of her physical attributes or because she had a charming personality, but there were always lots of guys hanging around her cart, which didn't seem to bother her boyfriend. This made me mildly suspicious, and then one day my suspicions proved true.

My partner and I were watching the row from our car at our usual corner when we saw Tammi and her boyfriend stop their cart at the corner across the street. We didn't pay them any special notice until a few minutes later after a considerable crowd of male skid row regulars had gathered around, which prevented us from seeing what was going on. Anytime there was a sizable crowd and the drunks started debating world issues or whose bottle was whose, it was a guaranteed fight.

22

S E X

My partner and I climbed out of our car, strolled across the street, then elbowed our way through the crowd, which was noisy with cat calls and cheers at whatever was going on in the middle. When we got to the clearing, it was instantly apparent why Tammi was so popular.

While her boyfriend stood by with a big grin on his face, Tammi sat perched in the cart with her dirty sweatshirt bunched up under her chin, exposing her breasts. Every few seconds a wino would step forward with a big shit-eating grin on his face and have himself a feel of those breasts. Tammi would just giggle and act like she was performing a service to the down-and-outers, which in a way she was. The men acted quite manly after their feel and seemed content to walk on and conduct their business.

Our guess was that Tammi's boyfriend was collecting a dollar or two for his girlfriend's services, but since we never witnessed it, we just broke up the group and scooted them along.

Everyone was mad at us for interfering, especially those guys who hadn't had their turn yet.

THE NAKED DANCER

My partner Karen and I spotted a large crowd on the corner about a block ahead of us. "Something is up," I said, pointing out the obvious.

"Fight, probably," Karen said, retrieving the mike and informing radio that we would be out on an unknown problem. We got out of our car and nudged our way through the skid row regulars, all of whom were cheering and clapping at whatever was going on.

"What do you think, Officer?" a toothless 80-year-old man asked, pointing to a nearly naked 200-pound dancing woman. "Purty thing, ain't she?" His eyebrows were bobbing like humping caterpillars.

The "purty" thing was a middle-aged woman who was no stranger to the food line. Huge rolls of fat encircled her waist and hung down over her soiled panties. Her breasts were monstrous—at least 50-inchers, my partner later guessed. She was doing sort of a Hawaiian hula/funky chicken dance for the merriment of about a hundred street people. She had an enormous smile on her face, and that other look that some mentally disturbed people have. Several guys were clapping rhythmically and chanting, "Take off your panties, take off your panties."

Karen was a petite officer, except when she got pissed. Then she grew to six feet, four inches in a quick second. This was one of those times. "Get out of the way, you fucking pervert," she said to a big guy blocking her way. He must have hesitated a second because he was suddenly launched forward about 10 feet to the other side of the dance clearing, where he was caught by a couple guys, thus saving him from landing on his face.

Karen stepped up to the woman and, in a gentle voice, said, "Come on, Sweety. Come with me. Where are your clothes?"

"Never did see her with no clothes," a man in the crowd said. "She just walked around the corner the way she is now. Never seen her before, neither. Sure wish she'd take off those panties."

I quickly distracted Karen from punching the guy out by telling

24

her to take the woman's arm, and we began escorting her over to our car, much to the disappointment of the fans. There were lots of calls to "Let her dance!" and I could tell that Karen was making a mental note to jerk those guys around later. We put her into the backseat, and I retrieved a blanket from the trunk while Karen tried to talk to her. But the woman only smiled and looked out the windows at the faces peering in.

We drove a couple blocks away from the voyeurs so we could discuss what we were going to do with her. To make the decision easy for us, the woman started to babble things straight from another planet and, after a few minutes of that, we decided to make the 20-mile drive to the state mental hospital. We didn't handcuff her, which is always a mistake.

She kept the blanket over her through town but as soon as we got on the freeway she pulled it away. I pulled over, and Karen got in the back seat to cover her up, telling her in a motherly tone to keep the blanket over her. Karen got in front again, and I drove back into traffic.

I had been concentrating on the heavy commute and hadn't glanced in the back for a couple miles, when Karen suddenly blurted, "Oh my God." She was looking bug-eyed through the Plexiglas shield.

I jerked around, thinking that the woman had probably pulled the blanket off again, and I was right. But she had also put one foot up on the right door frame and her other on the left, as she masturbated about a hundred miles-per-hour. "Let's get it on," she mumbled.

"Get your feet down!" Karen shouted, sounding like a scolding mother. "Stop that right now."

"Let's get it on," the woman muttered. Then more clearly, "Let's get it on, let's get it on, let's get it on." Then shouting, "Let's - Get- It - On!"

"What do you want to do?" I asked Karen. "We're about two miles from the exit."

"Hey, asshole! What are you looking at?" Karen had her head out her window. A double trailer truck was matching our speed as the driver looked down into our backseat, as well as his passenger, who must have been lying across the driver's lap. "Back off unless you want a ticket," Karen roared. I was concerned about the driver losing control and side-swiping us.

"Here's the exit," I said, zipping around the truck. "The hospital is just a couple of miles. Let's just get her there and out of our lives."

Five minutes later, the woman was still doing her thing and shouting, "Let's get it on," as we pulled into the hospital drive-up. It was a little hard to pull her from her trance, but we managed to get her out of the car, wrap her in the blanket and walk her into the hospital.

We filled out the paperwork and explained to the staff what we had. A half hour later as we made our way out the door, we could hear the woman's voice in the holding room: "Let's get it on. Let's get it on."

"Fun job, huh?" I said sarcastically to Karen as we climbed into our car.

She nodded. "Yeah. Hey, isn't 'Let's Get It On' a song? What group sang that?"

"That's a song, too?" I asked.

THE YELLOW BUS

The Northwest is known for its berries—strawberries, raspberries, boysenberries, huckleberries, and others. When I was a teenager, my buddies and I worked summers picking them. It was hard work and low pay, but we had a blast eating more than we picked. That was in the late '50s and early '60s. By the time the '70s rolled around, kids were too cool and sophisticated, or so they thought, to get their hands dirty in the berry fields. No matter how many ads the berry farmers placed in the newspapers, they were always short of pickers and lost money as their crops rotted on the vines.

Old man Jackson from Jackson Berry Farms, however, got the creative idea of getting winos to pick his crops. Somewhere, Jackson had acquired a big yellow school bus that he would use to transport winos from skid row to his fields, then back to the row again. It took him a while to figure out a system that worked with winos, since they are not the most reliable employees, but once he got it figured, it worked like a charm. This is how he did it.

Jackson would drive his bus into skid row around 2 A.M. each night and park it near the hub of street activity. Then, as if he had a carrot on the end of a string, he would entice the winos onto his bus with bottles of wine. They would drink themselves into unconsciousness, which was OK with Jackson, since he didn't want to fuss with them on the long trip out to the farms.

He would time the trip so that he pulled into the fields at sunrise, which is prime time for picking berries. He would shake the shanghaied winos awake and promise them another bottle of wine after they had picked for him. Jackson never planned on a long work day with the guys, since their DTs would begin to kick in after three or four hours and their work ethic would deteriorate to nonexistent. Once they were back on the bus, he would give them all a bottle and they would have a fun trip back to skid row.

This worked for everyone: Jackson got his berries picked, and the winos got a couple of bottles and a sense of contributing to America's work force. They actually strutted when they climbed off the bus, feeling good about putting in a day's work (actually, three or four hours) like real working stiffs. And speaking of stiffs . . .

There was one other person who benefited from Jackson's yellow bus. Kate was a 50-year-old wino/prostitute, or possibly a prostitute/wino, since no one knows for sure which came first, including Kate, since her alcoholic brain was so far gone. But she was sharp enough to recognize an opportunity, and she discovered a big one in Jackson's yellow bus.

As soon as that bus came to a stop, Kate would be on it in the blink of an eye and quickly set up shop in the back. Once the bus was loaded and everyone was chugging on their bottles, Kate would hang the "Open" sign out, so to speak.

"Sometimes the guys would line up in the aisle," remembers one skid row officer. "It was a party-like atmosphere as each man worked his way through the line to have a moment with the skid row madam. I don't know what she charged, probably 50 cents, if that much."

Some would argue that the yellow bus just perpetuated the problem on skid row. Others, including Farmer Jackson, the berry-picking winos, and businesswoman Kate, thought it was a pretty darn good thing.

PRESSED BREASTS

There used to be a lot of topless joints on skid row, probably because the rent was cheap for the owners. Some of the places were fairly nice, as far as topless joints go. But others were what you would expect to find in the armpit of the city. Most of the beat cops frequented the places to have a cup of coffee and write reports; occasionally, they would check out the dancers.

On one block there were two places called Eros I and Eros II. Both theaters showed porno movies, then every hour or so would break to bring out live dancers to prance about in the aisles and on the laps of customers. Eros I offered female dancers while Eros II presented male dancers between showings of gay movies. Laws were looser then, and dancers in both theaters would do just about anything for a big tip.

I was never in Eros II, but my training coach and I went into Eros I once in a while. The cashier at the front counter would greet us with a phony smile, then flip a switch under the counter, which he didn't think we knew about, to activate a flashing light out in the theater to warn the girls that the cops were on the premises. By the time we got through the turnstile and into the theater, the girls were dancing as innocently as nuns in the aisles. A couple times, though, we managed to get in before he could flip the switch, and we would walk into an orgy of a half dozen naked girls playing with a dozen elated guys. My training coach never took police action because I think he liked watching the spectacle too much.

One night I was working without a partner, although I had been given a ride-along, a 25-year-old law school graduate who was about to become an assistant district attorney. After a few minutes of conversation with the guy, it was obvious he was smart, but naive and lacking any real-world experience. We were the same age, but I had been in Vietnam and on the police job for about 15 months.

It was a busy night: One call would frighten him, the next would leave him in awe, and the next would confuse him as to the freakiness of the human condition, especially the unique human condition on skid row.

I had made a traffic stop in front of Eros I, then afterwards pulled

29

to the curb under the brightly lit marquee to catch up on some earlier reports. The sidewalks were busy with passersby, especially people going in and out of Eros I. My driver's window was up, and I was concentrating on a report and answering my ride-along's questions.

"Yoo hoo, Officer," a female voice called from the sidewalk.

I looked out the side window and saw an attractive woman walking toward the car from Eros' double doors. She was wearing a sweatshirt, and her breasts were swaying in total freedom underneath. I reached for the window crank, but before I could turn it even once, she pressed her chest against the glass.

"How are you tonight, Officer?" she taunted. Then she pulled up the front of her sweatshirt and pressed her bare breasts against the glass. "Oooo, this is cold," she cooed, rubbing her breasts up and down on the glass.

"Hey, knock that off!" I called out, quickly winding the window down. She backed away and giggled.

She turned around, flipped her hip at me and joined another woman who had just walked out of Eros I. "Have a nice evening, baby," she called over her shoulder. I could hear her laugh as she told her friend what she had done.

I glanced over at my ride-along as I chuckled and rolled the window up. His lower jaw was hanging as if broken. "Oh - my - God!" he coughed out. "I have never seen anything like that it my life. She exposed her breasts to you. She actually pulled her sweatshirt up and pressed them against your window."

I laughed and told him of another time on the job when a woman had done the same thing.

"You are kidding me. I can't believe it. I have never known anyone to have an effect on women like that."

"What?" I asked, not sure that I had heard him right.

"You must have women all over you all the time to have them just come up like that and show you their breasts."

I decided not to tell the naive guy that this had never happened to me away from the job. Let him have his opinion, I thought.

"Yeah," I said, trying to sound casual. "Sometimes it's a curse."

LOVE IN A DUMPSTER

"Dennis and I were partnered one night," tells Officer Tom Johnson, "and we were working a prostitution detail. We happened to pass by this big Dumpster that was at the side of a building on skid row, and we could see a guy inside of it. There was garbage strewn all over the ground as if he had been throwing it out. I told dispatch that we would be out checking on a Dumpster diver.

"We circled around the block and parked about 50 feet away. The guy was still inside the huge box, bent over at the waist and flailing his arms around; we assumed he was throwing the garbage out. We approached cautiously, so he remained unaware of us even after we were virtually on top of him.

"'What are you doing?' I asked loudly, looking over the wall of the Dumpster. He was still bent over and flailing his arms, though we had yet to see him throw anything out. It struck me that his arm flailing was sort of strange. My voice startled him and he jumped a mile, then just stood there dumbly like a kid who's been caught with his hand in the cookie jar.

"He was a typical-looking skid row person: wearing an army fatigue jacket, black stocking hat, with a dirty face and an overall filthy look. He was wearing OD army fatigue pants, too, which were bunched down around his knees. His fatigue jacket extended to about mid-thigh so we couldn't see his privates.

"'Pull up your pants,' I said. He tugged on them a little, but for some reason he couldn't get them up. Dennis asked for his identification and the guy searched the pockets of his pants, which had fallen back down. He was a pleasant enough guy, but he was definitely a hard-core street person. He gave me his ID and I told Dennis I would go back to the car and run him through the computer. Dennis stayed with the guy and watched him.

"He checked out OK, so I gave his ID back and asked him what he was doing in the Dumpster. That's when I noticed that he had pulled his pants up. Dennis said later that he must have done it when he looked away for a second. I also noticed something lying

31

on the ground between the man's feet that hadn't been there before. A shiny, wet dildo.

"Dennis and I looked at each other. I could see the dawn of realization happening in his face, and I'm sure he could see it mine. Now we knew why the guy had been acting so sheepish when we first tried to talk to him. He had been standing there with a dildo stuck in his butt, which had also kept him from pulling up his pants. Here is what we later pieced together based on what he said and what we observed.

"Apparently, the guy had nothing to do with the garbage strewn all over the ground. He had just been in the Dumpster having a little creative solo sex by wedging one end of the dildo into a crack in the Dumpster, then backing himself up to it and inserting the other end into his. When we saw him waving his arms about, it was just his way of expressing glee."

SHE'S PACKIN'

At least once a week in roll call, beat officers are given warrant cards for people residing in their area of patrol. Each card has the name of a person wanted for a particular misdemeanor or felony crime, as well as a physical description of the wanted person, including the last known address. By the time the cards are issued by the Warrants Division, however, the wanted person has usually moved away. Other times, the address doesn't even exist because the person just made something up when he was arrested. The cards are considered a pain by most officers, since they seldom result in an arrest.

Officers Cramer and Felton went to the Smithson Hotel to serve a warrant card. The hotel is about as scummy as they come on skid row, and the two officers never for a moment thought the wanted female wino would still be in there six months after her initial arrest. Cramer raised his hand to rap on the door, but stopped in mid air.

"Listen," Cramer said, putting his ear close to the door. "What is that?"

Felton leaned close and listened for a second. "Sounds like a woman moaning. Sounds like she's having . . . sex. And enjoying it. You've probably never heard a woman make those sounds before, huh Cramer?"

"Just from your wife," Cramer said, blank-faced. He banged on the door. The moaning stopped. He banged again.

"Who the fuck is it?" a female voice screeched from inside.

"It's the police," Felton called. "Open the door."

The officers heard the female voice say "Dammit!" followed by a scooting sound like a chair would make on a hardwood floor. They heard the door lock being released, then the door opened a few inches. "What the fuck you want?" the woman spat.

"Are you Viola Washington?" Cramer asked, nudging the door open with his shoe.

"Yeah, that's me. So fucking what?" A cigarette protruding from the corner of her mouth bobbed up and down with each word. She squinted a bloodshot eye through the smoke.

Cramer pushed the door open all the way and could see that Viola was only wearing a thigh-high bathrobe. "Who else is here?" Felton asked, thoroughly disgusted at what the years of booze and hard living had done to her.

"No one. I'm here alone." She reluctantly stepped aside as the officers crowded their way inside. They scanned the small room and saw that she was indeed alone. So what was up with the sounds? they both wondered.

"Get some clothes on," Felton said. "You're coming with us."

"Sons-of-a-bitch," Viola spat. "Well, just a second." Then, without a pittance of modesty, she opened her bathrobe and reached down between her legs. "Here," she said, pulling out a very long and very pink dildo. "You want this?"

Felton says that Cramer reached out and took it, but Cramer adamantly denies it.

PART TWO
VIOLENCE

Anything that can be defined as violence
happens on skid row. Some days it would seem that every other staggering person wore a head bandage, an arm cast, a leg splint, a back brace . . . sometimes all of the above. About half of the walking wounded had made the mistake of crossing horns with someone who didn't appreciate having their horns crossed, or they had tried to cross horns with a truck bumper that was passing through the row at 35 mph. Many of them were so drunk at the time of their injury that they couldn't tell you how they got hurt. "I woke up this mornin', Officer," a man would say, scratching his head, "and here's my damn arm in a cast. Must've hurt it last night, or somethin'."

Broken limbs and bloody wounds were often a form of identity, sort of a way of being somebody in a place where they were often looked at no differently than the debris the wind skittered along the filthy sidewalks. Like a small child with a Band-Aid-covered finger, a wino would walk with his plastered arm held out so that all could see his injury, or hobble along on crutches, looking at each passing face with the hope that someone would care enough to ask what happened. Usually, no one did.

Scabbed foreheads, swollen lips, and bleeding teeth were as common as makeup at a beautician's convention. Sometimes a guy's forehead would have scabs upon

35

scabs—fresh ones on old ones—the result of head-first falls. Swollen lips and bleeding teeth were either from falls or not ducking when another wino swung a bottle.

My guess is that there was a lot of painless death on the row. When a guy had a blood/alcohol ratio of about 50/50, he probably couldn't feel that knife slice through his kidney, that corner curb crack his skull, or that truck's bumper splinter his ribs. One moment he was staggering along in a thick, swirling fog, and the next moment the fog was swallowed by blackness. Some might say that if you've got to go, that's not a bad way to do it.

A lot of cops got hurt working there. If you worked the paddy wagon wrestling drunks every shift, you were just about guaranteed a sucker punch in the chops, a sprained finger, a blown-out back, and a few skinned knuckles. It could be a real challenge trying to hold your temper fighting winos and other skid row characters day after day. Sometimes you could, sometimes you couldn't . . .

FUN WITH PRISONERS

"The first thing we did every morning was to make a sweep of the usual crash sites where winos congregated overnight to drink, party, fight, puke, and pass out," says Officer Painter. "We would cruise the doorways, warehouse loading docks, freeway underpasses, and alleys. Some mornings there would be only a half dozen or so; other days, especially around the 1st and the 15th of the month when they got their government checks, there would be scores laid out as if struck down by a deadly plague.

"The detoxification center was a half mile away from the heart of skid row, so we would load one or two drunks into the backseat of our car and make a quick trip to dump them off. Some days we would make a dozen trips or more before noon. There would have been more, but after three hours, many of those we hadn't gotten to yet had awakened and staggered off.

"If we found three or four guys in a good mood and having a good time, we would squeeze them all in the backseat to save us a couple of trips. The happy drunks didn't mind the tight squeeze, and sometimes sang in unison all the way there.

"Then there would be the combative ones. Usually there would be two—sometimes even three or four—of them throwing wild punches and kicks at each other in a doorway, or a couple of them rolling around on the sidewalk mutually choking each other. They were too drunk to launch blows of substance and far too pickled to feel anything anyway. The humane thing, the logical thing, would have been to break up the fighters and call for another police car so they could be transported to the detox separately.

"But that wouldn't have been any fun.

"Fun was stuffing the fighters together in the backseat, sometimes handcuffed, sometimes not, then cruising the long way to the detox. No one was ever seriously hurt during these trips, since it was difficult at best to land a good punch in the confines of a police car's backseat, especially when the warriors had at least a .30 blood/alcohol reading. Occasionally, we would hear a fairly pronounced splat

37

against a jaw, but usually the ruckus would consist of cursing, bodies being pushed against doors, and heads slamming against the Plexiglas shield that protects the police in the front seat from the bad guys in the back.

"Sometimes the fighters would calm down after we crammed them into the back, so we would have to encourage them a little. 'So Willy,' my partner would say over his shoulder, 'You don't mind ol' Charlie there calling your mother a whore?'

"Willy would snap his head toward Charlie and say, 'What? You bastard! You called my mother a whore?' Willy would punch Charlie in the chops, and Charlie would respond by squeezing Willy in a headlock. Willy would curse and grab a handful of Charlie's groin and squeeze until Charlie sang soprano.

"And in the front seat, we were as giddy as school children."

VIOLENCE

WHOOPS!

I worked skid row first as a rookie and then returned 10 years later. The years in between, I worked in one of the outlying precincts that is far removed from skid row, though I still had to pass through the area to get to the main police station downtown. Such was the case one day when my partner, Joe, and I had to go to Personnel for some reason.

We had just come off the bridge and were passing by an old skid row tavern called the Seven Seas. My guess is that the place opened during World War II when the east and west shores of the Willamette River were chaotic with people and activity from the shipyards. The shipyards are no longer what they were during the war, but the Seven Seas still caters to the working man and the local winos.

Since the west side is on a different radio frequency than the east, we didn't know that an officer had called for cover at the Seven Seas until we saw him waving frantically at us as we passed the tavern. He was holding a junkyard shotgun in one hand and pressing a guy against the side of his police car with his other.

"Help me get this guy cuffed," Daniels said as Joe and I leaped out of our car.

We didn't know what had happened, but the fact that Daniels was struggling with a guy while holding a weapon that was not police issue was all we needed to know to dump the guy onto his belly and quickly get him cuffed. "What do you got?" I asked, after we chucked the prisoner in Daniels' backseat.

"Well, asshole here was walking into the Seven Seas with this shotgun in that carrying case," Daniels said, pointing to a cheap, vinyl rifle case lying on the curb. "He didn't want to give it to me, so we started dancing on the sidewalk. That's when you guys showed up. And he had these in his pocket." He showed us a box of shotgun shells. "I wonder if I could get you guys to take the shotgun to Property for me so I can run asshole to jail?"

"No problem," I said, reaching for the weapon. "You checked it?" Daniels was a range officer, and I knew he had, but you still have to ask.

"Yes, it's empty."

I looked into the chamber and double checked. It was a cheap shotgun, so when I tilted the barrel downward, the plastic slide moved forward and closed the port. Joe placed the box of shells into his coat pocket and handed me the carrying case, which was too big to go with the gun. I dropped the shotgun into it.

"OK, we're off. We'll leave the paperwork at the precinct front desk for you."

"Thanks," Daniels said.

We drove to the main station and found a parking spot in front. As we got out, I heard Joe curse. "Dammit! The bottom broke out of the box of shells. They're all over the sidewalk."

"Hey," I said teasingly, as I retrieved the shotgun off the backseat. "Take a Valium. Everything will be OK." I walked around to his side and unzipped the carrying case. "Just drop the shells into the case here and we'll check everything in as one package."

Since it was a Sunday, we had to stop at Records and ask one of the clerks to get a key and walk downstairs to Property with us. Chris was a new girl, probably a college student, so the supervisor gave her the assignment and a ring with a zillion keys. Joe and I bantered with her as she tried to find the right one to unlock the door that led to the basement. After a minute, I let out a dramatic sigh and leaned on the shotgun, the barrel end into the floor.

The roar was deafening and it seemed to echo through the halls forever. There was an unreality about it, and the three of us stood dumbly looking at the floor where the tile was shredded next to my right foot. I started laughing and the Records girl started howling. For a second, I thought she was laughing, too, but then I realized she was howling in pain as she clutched her butt.

That's when I felt a stinging sensation in my right shin.

"I must have gotten some powder burns," I said to Joe who was asking the Records girl if she was OK. I pulled up my uniform pants leg to check my skin—my leg looked like a sieve with hair. Later, the doctor counted 14 holes, but at the moment I just stared in disbelief at all the blood arcing from my shin. That's when the pain struck.

I plopped down onto my rear and held my leg as blood pumped

out onto the floor in every direction, not unlike a lawn sprinkler. Joe didn't know who to help, the howling Records girl, who we were to learn later took two pellets in her butt, or me, who had taken 14. He asked if I wanted an ambulance, and I told him no, though I definitely needed to go to a hospital. I just didn't want the attention an ambulance would bring. The Records girl refused an ambulance, too, and was led off by her supervisor to see her own doctor.

I may as well have taken an ambulance, since it turned out that everyone in the world came to the hospital anyway: sergeants, captains, deputy chiefs, and the chief. Of course they all wanted to hear the story and no matter how I tried to convince them, not one of them believed that the shotgun was unloaded when we put it into the carrying case.

The doctor dug ten pellets out of my shin and left four in, which are still there today. The Records girl had two removed from her butt, and Joe found two in his boot.

When we told our sergeant what had happened, he didn't believe us either and went to Property to conduct a little experiment. He dropped the shotgun shells into the top of the now shredded carrying case, as Joe and I had done at the curb, and to his amazement, three out of four times a shell entered the port. Then when the shotgun was turned barrel down, the cheap slide moved forward and chambered the round. He figured that some of the overlarge carrying case's extra vinyl material somehow pushed against the trigger when I turned the weapon upside down and leaned on it like a cane.

Yes, it sounds like B.S., but that's what happened.

DON'T LET US DISTURB YOUR GAME

"My partner and I were having a cup of coffee in the local hash house," says Officer Frederick, "when we heard the officer in our neighboring beat car shouting on the radio that he and his partner and some citizens were in a foot pursuit after a stabbing suspect. He said that witnesses told them the victim was in the Moose Bar on 5th.

"Red and I took a last sip of coffee and hurried out to our car. The Moose Bar was only a block away, so we were there in a second. At the same time, the guys in our neighbor car said breathlessly over the radio that they had the guy in custody. We told radio that we were going into the bar to check on the victim.

"The Moose Bar was a Wild West show of drunks, fights, blaring country western music, and an occasional stabbing and shooting. It's a 20-something meat market now, with hanging ferns and pretty people on the prowl. Fifteen years ago, however, it was a definite hard-hat area.

"Cigarette smoke and blaring Willie Nelson music practically knocked us down as we entered. The place was packed, as always, with every bar stool occupied and every table surrounded with three or four sad-looking drinkers. We stood at the door for half a minute to let our eyes adjust to the place and to get an overall view of who was there. Everything looked 'normal' for the Moose Bar, and we didn't see anyone looking like he'd been stabbed. We moved over to the bartender and waited for Fat Eddie to move down the bar to us.

"'Someone get hurt in here tonight, Fat Eddie?' I shouted over Willie Nelson.

"He shook his heavy jowls and looked around the place. 'Nothin' happenin' tonight, boys, that I'm aware of.'

"Fat Eddie looked like he wasn't lying, something he usually did to protect his customers. I nodded thanks to him and shouted in Red's ear that we needed to look around the place. We worked our way through the tables and shook hands with a few drunks who offered theirs in greeting. Five minutes later, we had worked our way to the back of the bar, where several guys were playing pool, and a few others were standing around waiting their turn. A couple guys nodded to us, while others pretended that we weren't there. Red spotted the victim and pointed.

"He was lying on his back on the other side of the table, staring up at the ceiling. It was José, a Mexican guy we would see occasionally drinking on the street. We pushed a couple pool players out of the way and knelt beside him. We thought he was dead at first; then we saw his chest moving. There weren't any marks or blood on his front, so we carefully rolled him over.

"There was a 12-inch-long butcher knife sticking out of the center of the guy's back. All we could see was the handle because the entire foot-long blade was buried in him. What we learned later from the citizens who were helping the other officers chase the suspect was that while José sat at the table drinking and watching the pool game, a Cuban guy came up from behind him and stabbed him. The Cuban struck downward with the knife, so that the blade slid down along his spine, destroying all the nerves and the spinal cord in its path. Later at the hospital, the X-rays showed the knife blade running parallel to his spine.

"José survived the stabbing, though he was paralyzed from his waist down. But it didn't slow him down much. He continued to live on skid row, rolling around the sidewalks in his wheelchair and becoming one of the area's active drug dealers, buying, selling, and holding dope for other Mexicans. One time I pulled a needle out of his arm after he had nodded off in his chair.

"He wasn't that old, but he died a couple years ago."

DON'T MIND ME, I'M JUST BLEEDING

The Club 101 was a notorious doper bar right in the heart of skid row. A few winos staggered in from time to time, but it was mostly a place where the harder element hung out to play pool and buy and sell narcotics. It was a dangerous place for a cop to go into alone, so usually two or more went in at a time and always kept their backs to the wall. But still things don't always go down the way one would like.

"Club 101 was an asshole place full of assholes, " says Officer Sanders. "I was driving by one day, checking out who was coming and going through the joint's front door. I was by myself and had no intentions of going in. There were more people than usual passing in and out, so I pulled to the curb, about two car lengths from the front door, just to sit and watch who was out on the street this day. That's when the guy staggered out the door.

"He was a hard-looking 25-year-old, not a wino but a tough street person. He waved one of his hands around like he was swatting flies, and clutched at his neck with his other hand where a big arc of blood spurted. He had just had his neck slit with a knife inside Club 101.

"I leaped out of my car and tried to get him to sit down against the side of the building. I grabbed his neck to apply pressure to the wound while at the same time yelling in my portable radio that I needed an ambulance. The guy was understandably panicky and was half fighting my efforts to help him. His blood was shooting into the air and splattering all over me as we stumble-danced around the entryway to the bar.

"This went on for probably six or seven minutes, while people just walked around us or brushed by us as they continued to enter and leave the place. Most didn't pay any attention, and those who did just gave us an indifferent look as they went about their business.

"After all, they had dope to buy and sell."

VIOLENCE

THE OPEN WINDOW

Big Jack, with his mop of white hair and a torso like a B-52 bomber, had patrolled the skid row streets seemingly forever. Virtually every rookie on the department had learned the ropes from Big Jack, and each one loved him, as did the people who lived and worked on skid row. Winos and other down-and-outers were all his special children, and they all knew it. But when one got out of line, he let them know that, too.

"I was a rookie working with Big Jack," says Officer Clemmons, now a 20-year veteran. "We got a call on a family fight at the Joyce Hotel, a real dive of a place on 4th Avenue. The desk clerk told us that the couple had been screaming at each other all morning and it had gotten to a point where it was no longer tolerable, which was saying a lot for a dive like the Joyce.

"We climbed the stairs to the third floor and could easily hear the couple yelling, though their room was at the far end of the long hall. We rapped on the door, but they didn't hear it because they were yelling so loudly. So, we beat on the door with the ends of our steel flashlights until there was a pause in the yelling. Then the female half opened the door.

"She would have made a witch look good: rotten teeth; dead, stringy hair; wearing just a Mickey Mouse T-shirt and the filthiest pair of panties I'd ever seen before or since. 'Take the fucker out of here,' she screamed, about two inches from my face. I stepped back reflexively and heard chuckling from Big Jack behind me. I was the puppy and he was letting me handle the call.

"The male half, who was perched on the edge of the bed, looked about as bad as the female. He wore only a pair of rotten shorts, one sock, and was as drunk as the witch. His bony chest was heaving from all the excitement but at least he was quiet. Then the asshole suddenly screamed incoherently and charged toward us. I started to go for my baton, but Big Jack, who never bothered with such accessories, stepped forward and stopped the charge with those big palms of his against the asshole's bird-like chest. That really pissed the guy off and he screamed that he was going to first kick our asses and then shoot us. Then the witch lunged at him, but I grabbed her arm and held her back. Asshole then tried to push his way past Big Jack to get to her, which was his biggest mistake that day—besides waking up.

"Big Jack's fist, which was as big as a beach ball, slammed into the man's jaw. His bare foot and his socked foot came off the floor as he catapulted backwards, across the bare floor, past the end of the bed, over the pile of clothes, and out the open, third story window.

"For the first time, the witch stopped screaming. Then what seemed like forever, the three of us just stood there in silence looking at the open window which the asshole had disappeared through a moment earlier. Big Jack's jaw was hanging slack, the most emotion I had ever seen him show.

"Shit,' I said, 'Aren't we on the third floor?'

"The witch hugged herself and wailed a mournful cry as Big Jack and I made our way over to the window, though neither of us really wanted to look out and see asshole splattered on the sidewalk far below. The only sound was our rapid breathing and the usual traffic noises outside, which seemed oddly normal.

"We stood before the window for a moment, each waiting for the other to lean over the yellow, paint-chipped sill. Finally, Big Jack made the move.

"Suddenly asshole's head bobbed up from the other side of the window. He looked past us toward the witch and screamed, 'I want that fucking bitch out of this room, Officers.'

"There was a fire escape landing about three feet below and asshole had landed on it, where he laid for a long moment, dazed from Big Jack's awesome punch. There was a trickle of blood coming out of his nose, but he was too drunk and too pissed at the witch to pay any mind to it.

"When asshole sprung up, Big Jack jumped a foot and so did I. We'd been convinced the guy was one with the concrete below and that we were in a heap of trouble.

"Big Jack grabbed him by his bony shoulders, dragged him through the window, and then down onto the floor. We cuffed him up while the witch screamed for us not to take him away. I even had to push her back a couple times, but not before I double checked that there was an inside wall behind her and not a window.

"I can't remember what we charged asshole with. Sometimes you have to get kind of creative with the statutes."

ERNIE BIGBEAR

Everything in life is relative, and unwanted tavern drunks are no exception. For example, a drinker considered an unwanted person in an uptown, upscale watering hole would be an acceptable drinker in a skid row tavern. A couple guys scuffling in a booth or in the men's room wouldn't draw a second look from a skid row bartender or any of the hard-drinking patrons, while such an occurrence uptown would be talked about there for weeks. An unconscious wino draped across a table top for hours would just never happen uptown, but it's considered part of the ambience on skid row.

My training coach and I got a call one night on an unwanted drunk disturbing at Red's Place, a filthy, hole-in-the-wall tavern.

"The guy must be really acting up for Red to call the police," my coach said. "He doesn't like us, and he definitely doesn't like us in his establishment."

I carefully steered the police car through the streets that were as busy as Mardi Gras. It was the first of the month, and the checks were in, so all the drunks were out of their minds. "There are a lot of Indians in Red's," my coach continued, "and most of them are still pissed about Wounded Knee. We have to watch each other's back."

I had been awarded my second-degree black belt in karate a few months earlier, and I loved skid row for all the real-life practice I got. I have never sought out fights on or off the job, because I have always respected the martial arts' tenets that say that force is to be used only as a last resort. But force has always been a large part of working skid row as a police officer, so I took advantage of the many opportunities working there to see what worked and what didn't.

There were a dozen people cluttering the door to Red's as we pulled to the curb. It was hard to say if they were just there as part of the natural scene or they had been chased out of the place because of whatever was going on inside. We quickly learned that it was the latter.

"Hey cops," a drunken voice boomed through the blaring western music that poured out the door. "You better do something with Bigbear. He gets real nuts when he's been drinking the firewater."

My coach and I exchanged looks as we pushed through the crowd. We were familiar with Ernie Bigbear, and we would have to agree that he did get nutso when he drank. A week earlier, we had fought him out of another tavern where he was trying to take on everyone in the joint. Wrist locks and armbars were insufficient force when it came to trying to control the man; the more pressure we applied to the pain holds, the more he smiled and the harder he fought. He loved—and I stress *loved*—to fight.

Happily, his stature didn't live up to his name. He was about five feet nine inches tall at maybe 170 pounds. But he was tough and possessed of an extraordinary warrior spirit that would have served him well back in the cowboy and Indian days. He had been in town from South Dakota for only a few weeks, which was the extent of what we knew about him, other than, as I've said, he liked to fight, and fight hard.

We whacked him with our batons the first two times we hauled him in. The blows slowed him down momentarily, but they never wiped that happy smile from his face. He would punch and kick and smile, even after four of us had gotten him down and a couple of the officers whipped him with their batons. We used our collective muscle to drag him inch by inch to the police car, while he grinned as if having the best time of his life.

As we cleared the doorway, we spotted him in the smoke-filled room, crouched like a college wrestler. He shot us a sweet smile, like old friends who have found one another in a crowd. He wasn't our friend, but I guess in his sadomasochistic mind, we were his. The two guys sprawled at his feet moaned so loudly that we could even hear them over the cowboy music.

Then Ernie Bigbear leapt at us.

It's always risky beefing with someone in a skid row tavern since the police are seldom welcome there. Not only must you concentrate on the task of controlling the resistor, but you must remain alert for one or more of his buddies dashing out from the shadows and sticking you with a knife or a broken bottle. That was not the case, however, when scrapping with Ernie Bigbear, since everyone hated and feared him so much. They just wanted us to get him out of the place.

We ran him, and he ran us, into chairs, tables, against the bar, and over it. He kicked and flailed, and we choked and thumped the dog crap out of him, but not once did he stop smiling. We eventually got him into the backseat, where he slammed his head into the side windows and the Plexiglas shield between the seats. By the time we had driven the 10 blocks to the jail, it looked as if he had spent his energy and gone to sleep.

He groggily let us help him out of the backseat, through the double doors, and down the hall to the elevator that would take us to the fifth-floor jail. I had just punched the button when a voice called out from behind us.

"Hold the door, hold the door." It was Officer Bob Allen with four winos in tow. "Got room for us on there?" he asked rhetorically as he guided his drunken charges ahead of him. "I'm giving my boys here a room for the night. They're cold and want to stay someplace cozy."

My coach guided our prisoner into the elevator and told him to face the corner. Then we helped Bob stuff his drunks into the small space, which added up to eight people in a space intended for five or six.

Ernie Bigbear decided to fight when the elevator doors swished shut.

His first move was to spin around and head butt Bob Allen in the face, which majorly pissed off the usually happy-go-lucky officer. He made a grab at Ernie, but two of his winos had slumped in between them and he ended up hitting one of the innocent drunks in the chops. My coach and I were slamming Ernie against the elevator wall, though not hard since there was no room to build up momentum. Somehow, our handcuffed prisoner was able to use his knee to hit both of us with a couple of solid blows. A third knee strike hit a wino, which woke and angered him enough to cause him to do a couple of body slams against Ernie. A few seconds later, the four winos and Ernie Bigbear were all fighting as ferociously as handcuffed men can fight in a jammed space.

Then the doors swished open, and every last one of us fell out onto the floor in a heap of flailing limbs. Somehow, in the pile, Ernie slipped his cuffed hands around to his front and was swinging them like a club, striking uniforms and winos as he climbed to his feet. Someone knocked him onto his back, and I moved in for a power punch that I hoped would knock Ernie into Tweety Bird land. Unbeknownst to me, however, Bob Allen had a similar plan, but his was to do it with a professional wrestling technique called "The Atomic Knee Drop."

A half second before my knockout punch was to connect with Ernie Bigbear's face, Bob's knee landed on the Indian's forehead. My fist followed, but slammed into the tender muscles of Bob's calf.

We all thrashed about for a few more seconds before a handful of jailers came to our assistance and established order to the mess. That's when I noticed that Bob Allen had crawled away and curled into a ball as he held his calf. "What the hell did you do that for?" he strained through clenched teeth. "I can't stand on it."

I apologized profusely as my coach and I helped him to his feet. "I'm supposed to go hunting tomorrow," he groaned. "I don't know if I still can. Man, it hurts."

POSTSCRIPT

Ernie Bigbear made the mistake of trying to fight a jail sergeant who had arms the size of Ernie's chest. The big sergeant toyed with him until he got bored, then grabbed Ernie by his hair and repeatedly banged his head into the floor until he lost consciousness. The sergeant then strapped him into a gurney and pushed him to the top of a long ramp that led down to the jail area. He gave the gurney a nudge that sent it rocketing down the ramp, at least 25 miles per hour. It came to an abrupt stop when Ernie's head hit a jail bar.

Bob Allen had to cancel his hunting trip because of his injured calf muscle. No amount of apologizing from me could restore his usual happy face.

Twenty years later, Ernie Bigbear suddenly reappeared in town, and a few days later became involved in a running gun battle with a security guard through the streets of downtown Portland. He killed the guard, and after a brief car chase, surrendered to the scary end of a police officer's shotgun.

I'LL KEEP AN EYE
OUT FOR IT

I was working by myself one day when I got a call on two winos fighting in an empty lot. Although it took only a couple of minutes for me to get there, I found only one man, and he was down on all fours in the dirt.

I canceled my backup and walked over to the old wino, who was moving around with his head close to the ground like a dog sniffing for whatever it is they sniff for.

"How you doing today?" I asked, kicking away an old, yellowed page of newspaper that had blown up against my leg.

The old-timer didn't answer, but continued rooting around and patting patches of grass that dotted the debris-strewn lot.

"Were you in a fight?" I asked, watching him curiously.

"Yeah," he growled drunkenly, without looking up. "We were a fightin' some."

"Are you OK? You hurt?" I still hadn't seen his face.

"Nope." Then a moment later, "Yup, back of my head hurts some."

"Do you need an ambulance? What do you need?"

"I," he said, still patting tufts of grass.

I waited for him to say more, but he didn't.

"Sir? What is it you need?"

"I."

My patience was beginning to thin. "'I' what? What is it you want?"

"Dammit," he said, looking up at me. "I need my eye." He jabbed his thumb toward his face. "I'm a lookin' fer my eye." Inside the concave of where his left eyeball should have been was a partially open slit, exposing pink, wet meat. His one eye looked at me drunkenly, then rolled back to the ground to continue searching for its companion.

My last cup of coffee came up in a silent and sour burp. "Your eye?" is all I managed to say.

VIOLENCE

He dog-walked over to a pile of garbage and began poking through it. "The sons-of-bitch hits me from behind with that wine bottle over there." He pointed toward a half-empty bottle of Mad Dog 20/20 lying a few feet away. "Hits me right in the back of the head. Knocked my glass eyeball clean out." He brushed a flattened milk carton out of the way. "It gots to be around here somewheres."

SKID ROW
BEAT

A ROSE FOR A WINO

The armbar is a common jujitsu technique used in police work to take a combative person to the ground. It can be executed slowly, or it can be executed with extreme prejudice—hard enough to make an imprint in concrete.

Imagine that you are standing at a person's right side and facing the same direction he is. Grip his wrist with your right hand, and pull it up and across your chest. Roll his wrist so that his elbow points upward. Place your left wrist across his upper arm, about an inch above his elbow and pull up slightly on his wrist as you simultaneously press downward against his upper arm. This bends him at his waist. When you swing your right foot behind you and continue to press against his upper arm, the person will be forced around in a circle as his own momentum takes him to the ground and onto his belly.

One day, Karen and I pulled to the curb to check on a guy sleeping like a baby on the sidewalk. He was a little guy, wearing a red stocking hat and a shabby, too-large gray overcoat. We got him to his feet, though he acted like he would rather have pushed the five-minute snooze button. He tried to get away from us, but I took hold of his right arm and Karen grabbed his left. That is, I thought she had it.

I held his elbow and started to reach around to pat down his waist for weapons. I felt him make a funny movement with his left arm, then I saw his left hand moving in a fast arc toward me, a hand that gripped a full bottle of red wine. Karen told me later that she hadn't taken his arm, though I pretty much had that figured out when I saw that bottle getting closer to my face.

I instinctively jerked his wrist up to my chest and slammed my forearm against his elbow. My quick plan was to bend him over and spin him in a circle all the way to the sidewalk, a movement straight out of the how-to-do-an-armbar book. I spun him so hard that his feet virtually left the sidewalk as his momentum propelled him in an accelerating circle around me. He was about three quarters of the way around when I suddenly remembered something I hadn't considered during the heat of the moment. We had been dealing with

54

the wino right next to our police car, about three feet away. Taking the guy to the sidewalk was not going to happen because he was too close to our car, and at the speed he was moving, there was no way I could stop him.

Portland, Oregon, is known as The Rose City, and at one time someone came up with the brilliant idea of putting a large picture of a rose on the side of the police cars. My man's head hit that rose at about 20 mph, the impact making a gosh-awful sound, not unlike the splat! a watermelon makes when dropped from a second-story window.

Despite the velocity and the horrific sound, he didn't bloody the rose, though he did crumple to the curb like a ragdoll, where he whimpered for a moment, then laid silently. I rolled him onto his back and Karen pried the bottle from his fingers just as his eyes fluttered open. He grimaced from the pain that almost visibly radiated from his forehead.

"You didn't have to do that, Officer," he groaned.

"Well, you didn't have to swing that bottle at me." I looked up at the car door and noticed there was a slight indentation on the rose.

"Sorry, Officer," he said, reaching for his head.

"Besides," I said, as we helped the now mellow man stand on his wobbly legs, "I didn't do it. The car door did."

"Oh." He squinted at the car. "Kinda messed up your rose, huh."

"Yes you did," Karen said as we helped him into the backseat for his ride to the detox. "But we're not going to press charges."

He grimaced again at his throbbing head. "Thank you, Officers."

"You're welcome," Karen and I said.

JUST SITTIN' IN THE SUN

Hot summer days on skid row are usually busy in the mornings, after the drunks have awakened from their booze-induced unconsciousness, and in late afternoon after the sun has passed over the tall buildings and covered the row deep in shadow—a time when the alcohol and heat have turned the drunks mean.

Drunks like the shade, just as sober people do, but sometimes they are so pickled that they lean against a hot brick wall, slide slowly to the sidewalk, and lay there for hours, getting a burn that vacationing rich folks pay thousands for in the Caribbean. If no one complained, we would sometimes let drunks sleep it off wherever they happened to fall. In harsh weather, hot or cold, we scooped them up for the sake of their health and took them to the detoxification center where they would spend a few hours out of the elements.

Karen and I were cruising down a skid row back street one stifling summer afternoon, on our way to a parking lot we knew to have shade. The streets were an oven set on broil, where not a soul stirred. The radio was dead, and all we wanted to do was get into the shade and savor our Big Gulps.

We both saw the lone figure at the same time, sitting against a wall in the afternoon sun three blocks away. He was easy to spot since there was no one else in sight on the long stretch of sidewalk. I slowed as we came near. "Let's see what this dude is up to," I said, pulling to the curb and lowering my window. "What's up, bud—"

"What is he doing?" Karen said in my ear as she leaned over the radio console that divided our seats. It was a rhetorical question, because it was obvious.

The guy looked too healthy to be a wino. He was a clean little man, about 40, shirtless, shoeless, wearing only blue jeans. He was clean except for all the blood that poured from long, deep looking gashes on his arms, neck, chest, stomach, face, and hands. It's unknown how long he had been sitting there and how long he had been slicing his body with the jagged piece of glass, but judging by the many cuts and the volume of blood, it had been for quite a while.

He was in the process of drawing the glass slowly across the length of his forearm when I had called to him. He raised his eyes toward me, but he continued to make the steady slice. Blood gushed in the wake of the glass, though his face gave no indication of pain.

"Hey! Stop that!" I called out as Karen and I scrambled from the car. We fanned out and approached him diagonally from left and right. "Put down the glass," I said, my hand resting on my gun butt. "Put it down, now!" His eyes looked at me, puzzled, as he withdrew the glass from his arm, but then he quickly forgot me and began making a slice across his upper chest.

Karen and I both lunged and grabbed his arms. He struggled a little, but he was too weak from having lost so much blood to put up a good fight. We removed the glass from his hand, slapped on the handcuffs, and then held him down until the ambulance came.

"That was really gross," I said later, driving to a service station where we could wash off the blood.

"Agreed," Karen said, picking up her Big Gulp. "Damn! All my ice melted."

BEAT

ICEMAN

There is a fish-packing business in the China Town section of skid row where, several times a week, large trucks bring in tons of fish to unload on a side street dock. The trucking companies use shaved ice—tons of it—to keep the fish fresh during the long rides from wherever to the dock. Sometimes, when the packing house is the last stop on their delivery routes, they dump the ice in piles that are often five feet high in the Truck Loading Zone next to the building. In the summer, it melts in a couple days, but during a winter cold streak, it can take weeks.

One winter day, a fellow officer got a call on a dead body on the street next to the fish packing plant. When he got there, he found a dead wino, his head protruding from a pile of ice in the No Parking Zone. There were other piles along the block, so it was impossible to determine what truck dumped the ice or even when it was dumped.

Apparently, the wino was either lying on the curb, where the driver couldn't see him, or maybe he staggered up behind the truck just as the ice was being dumped. Whichever the case, he ended up on the bottom of a pile that sat unmelted for at least a couple of weeks. When the weather turned warmer, the ice began to slowly melt, revealing the ice-cubed wino underneath.

NO MORE TROPHIES

All I wanted to do was get through my Friday shift on time so I could go home and rest for my tournament on Saturday. I had been on a winning streak for about five years, bringing home more than 50 trophies from large and small karate tournaments throughout the Northwest. I had been training extra hard for about three months for Saturday's competition, since I had won it the year before and wanted to claim the title again. Yes, it was an ego thing.

I was always paranoid the week before a tournament that I might get hurt and not be able to compete. The week had involved a couple of minor scuffles with winos and a brief foot chase. Nothing big, but my worry needle was blipping into the red zone. So far, I had survived four days and seven hours, and all I had to do was get through 60 more minutes to be home free.

I was in the left lane of a one-way street approaching a busy intersection. As I slowed for the red light, I was aware of a flurry of movement to my left, and I turned just in time to see a man drive an ice pick into the side of another man's head. I shouted into the mike for a backup car and bailed out just as the stabbing victim crashed to the sidewalk.

There was a series of ornate metal posts about three feet high along the curb that served to support a chain barrier. It was a turn-of-the-century decoration that served no purpose that I could see other than to trip the blind drunks who staggered by 24 hours a day.

I hopped over the chain, grabbed the guy with the pick and dumped him hard onto his rear. I started to move in to disarm him, but amazingly, the bleeding victim leaped to his feet and kicked the stabber square in the face. I grabbed the victim and swept out his feet, plopping him down onto his butt. The stabber kicked at him from where he was lying on his back, and the victim tried to grab his feet. I could hear a siren approaching up the side street, and it couldn't get there any too soon as far as I was concerned.

The stabber again got to his feet, so I gave him a hard nudge that sent him sprawling under the chain and into the gutter. I would have drawn my weapon since he still had the ice pick, but the victim, who must have been too pissed to realize he was near death, grabbed my leg. That's when my backup screeched to a stop.

Edwards jumped out and immediately pulled the stabber to his feet, oblivious to the ice pick in his hand. I kneed the victim in the head, then took a giant step toward Edwards, yelling, "Knife!" I was on the sidewalk and the stabber was on the street side of the chain barrier. I reached across the barrier and grabbed a handful of the man's hair, twisted it and jerked him over backwards. This is a technique we used to teach in the academy and normally one that works like a charm because of the combination of pain and leverage. I had used it many times because it always accomplished the goal without causing injury, though it hurts like the dickens while it's happening. It worked this time, too, but I had to stretch out awkwardly to reach the guy, nearly falling over the chain in the process.

I instantly felt a funny sensation in my shoulder and upper chest.

The armed man crashed onto his back and Edwards was on him like a cat on a rat to remove the pick from his hand and to get him cuffed. I wrestled my victim into cuffs, too, and called for an ambulance. He may have been too dumb to know he was hurt, but the blood was really pumping out of his temple.

My arm was starting to grow numb; I knew something had happened to it. By the time the ambulance arrived, I couldn't open my hand, and I could barely move my arm The pain was excruciating. I got another unit to take my prisoner so I could do a one-handed drive back to the station.

That evening I went to the hospital and learned that I had separated a pectoral muscle and injured my deltoid. There would be no tournament the next day.

For the next several weeks I was in a sling and had to work a desk. I was eventually able to train again, but not at the extreme level needed for competition.

The officer never thanked me for dumping the armed guy, the victim never pressed charges, and I was never again able to compete in tournaments.

GYPSY: SHE'S A MAN EATER

She called herself Gypsy and was probably the best looking 20-something female on skid row, at least for the first few months until wine, beer, heroin, and sex with countless derelicts turned her into a crumpled replica of what she once was and would never be again. She stood about five-feet eight inches and was initially trim with a pretty face and a mop of beautiful, pampered hair. Within three months, all that faded and she became just another staggering, bloated alcoholic, albeit a popular one with the boys.

She tried kissing up to all the skid row cops, especially the young ones, forgetting that she had lost her looks to the debauchery of the street. Her attempts never worked and she always found herself sleeping it off on a wet cement floor in the detoxification center. I took her there several times, and, other than having to put up with her constant chatter, the trip was always without incident.

One hot summer day, my partner and I saw her walking along the sidewalk talking loudly and waving her arms around. She was obviously on something, but no worse than the others who were feeling their substance abuse. "Gypsy is feeling her oats today," I said to my partner, Warner.

"Yeah, she's loud already, and it's not even noon. Maybe she will crash somewhere and we won't have to bother with her." We decided to let her carry on and that we would check her out every time we drove past the corner.

During the next couple passes we didn't see Gypsy and had almost forgotten about her, when around 1 P.M. we passed the corner and saw her arguing with a tall, backpack-wearing transient. He was just standing dumbly while she screamed like a banshee at him, so out of it that we couldn't understand anything she was saying and it was doubtful the backpacker could either. He probably had made a sexual suggestion to her and, being new in town, had no idea that when she was on a trip, she was not open to sexual advances. But he was learning quickly.

"Hey Gypsy," Warner called from his window. "Knock it off right now, or you're going to spend this sunny day at the detox."

61

She jerked her head toward us and smiled, though her eyes looked insane. "OK, I'm outta here." She looked at the backpacker and said something we couldn't hear, then nudged him aside with her shoulder as she stormed off.

Warner shook his head, saying, "I have a feeling we're going to have to take her before this day is over."

"I think you're right," I said. And two hours later our guess proved accurate.

By 3 P.M. she was higher than a kite. We were crawling along the curb toward the intersection when we spotted her in the crosswalk, screaming and swinging at anyone who passed her by. She had lost her shoes and socks somewhere, though it didn't keep her from kicking at people. Lots of street folk had gathered on opposite corners of the intersection to watch the show, and traffic had stopped, unable to get around her—or afraid to for fear of getting their doors kicked.

"OK, that's enough," Warner and I said simultaneously as he pulled to the curb. "Let's take her," I said. "She's gone over the top now."

We climbed out and worked our way through the crowd. "Hey Gypsy," I said, stopping a few feet from her. "Come here."

"I ain't goin' no wheres with you guys," she blared. She swung at an elderly man passing by her, just narrowly missing him.

Warner and I moved toward her, though I was a step or two in front. Just as I moved into range, she swung wildly at me with a punch that would have made John Wayne proud. I saw it coming and jerked my head back, but still she clipped the tip of my nose. I swept her arm past me and continued pushing it around her neck until she was choking herself with her own biceps. Even as a veteran martial artist, I can't say what the heck I thought I was doing, other than it seemed like the thing to do at the moment. By pushing on her arm against her throat, I had her controlled, but it placed my wrist directly in front of her mouth.

The opportunity was not missed by Gypsy and she chomped into my lower forearm.

"Hey, she thinks your arm is a Big Mac," Warner blurted, in keeping with his usual warped perception of things. He grabbed at Gypsy as I howled in pain, but not before she took a second bite. He

62

slung her against a parked car as I bent over in pain, holding my bleeding arm. "You OK?" he called to me.

"No," I said with a grimace. "Damn, it really hurts."

Warner got her cuffed and began pushing her toward our back door. She made a feeble attempt to kick at me, which is all it took to blow steam out of my Pissed-Off Meter. I lunged at her, grabbed deep into the roots of her hair, and ran her into the side of our police car, three times. All I could think of was that she was a heroin user, a skid row prostitute, and she had to be infected with AIDS. And that now I had it.

She snapped out of her fit after becoming one with the side of the police car, and she began apologizing as the tears rolled down her cheeks. "I'm sorry I bit you. OK? I'msorryI'msorryI'msorry."

"Too late," I said, forgetting my neutrality. I jerked open the back door, then yanked her by her hair so that her bugged eyes were looking into mine. "If I have AIDS, you filthy piece of shit, I will hunt you down and kill you in a most painful way." Then I threw her into the backseat. We took her to jail and wrestled her out of the car and into booking. Before we put her into the holding cell, I reiterated my threat to hunt her down and kill her slowly. I could tell by her expression that she was taking me seriously.

From jail we drove to the closest hospital emergency room to have blood samples taken and to see if I had been infected. The doctor called me a week later to say the tests were negative for HIV, but that I should be tested again in a few months since the virus doesn't always show itself right away. Six long and anxious months later, my test again showed negative.

We rarely saw Gypsy after that. Whenever I did run into her, she took off like a bat out of hell. I heard from street people as well as other skid row officers that she was living in fear that I was really going to kill her. Well, I had no intentions of doing it, although if I had gotten infected, I'm not so sure.

At this writing, Gypsy is serving time in prison for being an accomplice in a murder.

WHEN JIMMY DISS'D CHIEF'S

Chief's Tavern slumps right in the middle of skid row. Ninety percent of its clientele are American Indians, many of whom are late-stage alcoholics, while the remaining 10 percent are there just to knock back a few beers and catch up on gossip. Chief's has been at the same corner forever and is known far and wide among the local Indian folk as a place where they can mingle with their own. Other races can drink there without being harassed, but it's important they keep in mind that it's an Indian drinking hole and respect it as such.

One time a dumb white guy went in there with the wrong attitude and diss'd the place.

Jimmy had drifted into town a week earlier and had been doing most of his drinking on the street, in doorways, and in a few taverns that catered mostly to whites. Then one afternoon he staggered into Chief's, no doubt drawn by the pungent aroma of spilled beer, fresh and stale cigarette smoke, and fresh and stale regurgitation.

He walked in from the bright sunlight into the dimly lit, smoky tavern and took a seat at the far end of the bar. He ordered a beer, apparently not noticing that the female bartender was obviously Indian. After a couple of sips, his eyes started to adjust, and that's when he noticed he was surrounded by them: there were Indians to his left, to his right, perched all along the bar, at tables all around the room, and two of them were sleeping like babies in a rear booth.

"Well Jesus Christ!" Jimmy blurted after his eyes took it all in and his pickled brain had registered what he was seeing. "There sure are a whole shitload of fuckin' Indians in here!"

Karen and I got there about a minute after we got the radio call, and ol' Jimmy was still unconscious on the sidewalk in front of Chief's. She waited outside for the ambulance and I went inside to get everyone's official denial. Of course, you would never have known anything had happened by looking around in the tavern.

People were chatting serenely and carrying on as usual. A couple of them even waved and smiled at me.

Two weeks later, I ran into the bartender when she was off duty and away from her peers. She told me all that I've related here, as well as the names of those who cold-cocked Jimmy and tossed his unconscious body out onto the sidewalk. It didn't matter, though, since he told us at the hospital that he didn't want to press charges. He said that once he got his jaw wired, he just wanted to leave town and "get far away from all those fuckin' Indians."

KNOCKIN' AT DEATH'S DOOR

My partner and I were sitting in our patrol car about a half block away from Chief's watching a hype pace back and forth on the sidewalk. He was about 22 years old, though he looked as if he had lived about 40 years on the mean streets doing exactly what he was doing now: looking to score juice for his hype needle.

"Want to check him out?" I asked Will. "Nothing else going on."

Will was sitting low in his seat, eyes half shut as the afternoon sun beat against his window. But with Will, half shut meant half open. He was watching the guy, too. "Let's wait and see who brings him his dope. It might make for a bigger bust."

About five minutes later, a half dozen people had gathered between the hype and us, so that we lost sight of him for a minute. When the crowd dissipated, the guy was gone. "Hey, where's our boy?" I asked. "You see him leave?"

"No," Will said, opening his eyes a little wider. "Oh well, we probably lost him."

"Maybe he went into Chief's. Couldn't get heroin, so he's settling for beer."

A few minutes passed and we were about to resume patrol when a man burst out of Chief's, waving frantically at us. "Police! Police! A guy in here just died!"

Will scooted up, eyes all the way open. He told radio what we had and that we were going in.

We pushed our way through the crowd that had gathered at the door and made our way into the dark tavern. It took a moment for our eyes to adjust, but when they did, we saw our hype curled into a ball on the floor next to the men's room. A couple of old drunks were standing next to him, leaning against each other and looking down, not knowing what to do. Others at the bar and at the tables kept right on drinking without at a glance at the man.

"What happened?" I asked, kneeling next to the guy. "Who saw

66

what happened?" I heard Will behind me tell dispatch to send us an ambulance.

"Officer," slurred one of the old drunks. "He just ran in here and went right into the shitter, then a bit later he came out and fell right there where you see him. Is he dead?"

"There's a hype needle on the floor," Will called from the rest room door.

And there's blood coming down his arm," I said. "He must have scored with someone when we couldn't see him. He's breathing, though—barely."

We stayed by the hype's side until the ambulance showed about five minutes later. No one was bothering him, anyway, since only the two old drunks were paying him or us any attention.

"What do you have" the female Emergency Medical Technician (EMT) asked, as she and her male partner kneeled.

"OD, most likely," I said, then told her what I knew.

For the next few minutes, the EMT people worked frantically to save the hype's life. They hooked up wires to his body, read meter information into a phone to someone at the hospital, slapped his face, took blood pressure readings, and talked more into the phone. I heard pieces of their conversation: " . . . isn't coming around . . . must have shot a big load . . . doesn't look good . . . isn't responding."

The female EMT looked up at me and shook her head. "I'm not sure if he is going to come out of it. We're going to shoot him with Narcan and see if that snaps him back."

Narcan is used frequently by emergency medical people to reverse the effects of a drug on an overdosed victim. It's sort of a "jump start." Since the victim is brought back from "death's door," the EMTs insist they be hospitalized for observation for at least 24 hours afterward.

Five minutes later, the hype started moving. His eyes fluttered open and he looked around dumbly. "Can you hear me?" the female EMT asked. "Do you know where you are?"

"Mmmph," is all the hype moaned.

"What drug did you shoot?" She got only another moan in response.

"OK, listen," she said into his face. "You almost died and we shot you with Narcan to bring you around. We have to take you to the hospital for observation. Understand?"

The hype kept widening his eyes, as if he were waking up from a deep sleep, which in a way he was. He shook his head and stumbled to his feet, though the EMTs insisted he stay down. They tried in vain to get him to go to the hospital, but he vigorously shook his head. We ran a check on his ID and he checked out OK, so we had no choice but to let him go.

"You guys really need to watch him," the female EMT said, as the hype walked unevenly out the door. "He was near dead; we just barely brought him back."

Five minutes later we were back in our car. We knew that Narcan negated the heroin the hype had shot and that he was going to be hungry again. We pulled out into traffic and rounded the corner and, sure enough, there was our man.

Oblivious to us, he again was pacing the sidewalk, looking desperately at each passerby who just might have a little something to sell him.

RIGHT IN THE KISSER

One time I was standing outside the door of Chief's talking to a man named Orville about a problem he was having. The man was sober, and I was giving him some tips on how to get help at the Social Security office. It was a Saturday, and the sidewalk was more crowded than usual with winos and a few straight citizens who would cut a fast path through the area on their way to a weekend carnival in a nearby park just outside skid row.

I hadn't been in Chief's that day, but judging by the sound of loud talking and laughing, I assumed the place was packed. We were standing to the side of the door as customers passed in and out, sometimes saying hello, sometimes just nodding.

I had been talking to the man for about five minutes when the biggest Indian in the history of skid row walked out into the light. Brownmoose was monstrously fat with arms the size of Ford truck tires, a belly the size of the truck cab, and braided hair that reached his butt. I had talked to him a few times and found him to be a decent sort.

He squinted against the sun, looked at me and nodded a greeting, then drove his fist, which was the size of the Ford pickup's hood, into Orville's face.

It made a bone crunching sound that I can still hear today, and Orville went flying across the sidewalk, over the trunk of a car, and down onto the street. "What the heck are you doing?" I shouted at the big Indian as I ran over to Orville. "Why did you hit him?"

"It's personal, Officer. Somethin' between Orville and me."

I slapped Orville's cheeks a couple of times and called his name. I was just getting ready to order an ambulance when his eyes fluttered open. "Hi," he coughed. His eyes were fogged over and half crossed.

"Are you all right?" I asked.

Orville shook his head a couple of times. "Yes, I think so."

"You want to press charges against Brownmoose?" I asked, looking at the big Indian who was just standing there with no expression on his face.

69

"No, no . . . it's OK. It's just personal. Something between him and me."

"You sure?"

"Yes."

"OK," I said, and nodded to Brownmoose that he could go.

He nodded a good-bye, turned, and went back inside Chief's.

VIOLENCE

THE WRESTLER AND THE CAR DOOR

On Dawn Street there was a tavern that had probably been there since the turn of the century. It had gone by many names over the years but was now called the Five Fifty-Five Club—thought up by someone either very clever or very unimaginative, since 555 was the tavern's address. Poor lighting gave it a dreary atmosphere, a 30-foot ancient bar gave it potential, and perhaps most interesting were the wood floors, which had been worn down by 60 years of stumbling feet, spilled beer, splattered blood, and a million squashed cigarette butts. I had been there dozens of times to break up fights and wrestle mean drunks out the door, and so had every other downtown police officer who had pounded a beat on Dawn Street over the last 60 years.

I was working by myself and was only a few blocks away when I got a radio call on an "unwanted drunk," at the Five Fifty-Five Club, my third that week. The neighboring beat car said he would back me up.

I rounded onto Dawn, which is a busy, four-lane street, and saw three or four people on the sidewalk peering into the open door of the Five Fifty-Five Club; something was definitely going on.

I stopped one door down from the club and parked in the No Park Zone in the curb lane. I waited until there was a break in the passing traffic that was struggling to maneuver around me, then I dashed from the car to the curb. That's when I heard a roar from inside 555. It was a human sound, yet so animalistic that it sent the spectators scattering to the far corners of the block. Another unearthly roar came from inside, followed by a couple drinkers dashing out the door and down the sidewalk. A moment later, the source of the jungle sounds burst out the door, stopping about 15 feet from me.

I was to learn later that Bruno had been a big-name professional wrestler until booze ruined his career and eventually sent him on a one-way trip to skid row. But he was still a monster, capable of crushing any bathroom scale that didn't have numbers higher than 350. He was fat, but that kind of solid fat that strong men have— men who work in construction, or compete in power-lifting contests, or throw other men over ropes.

He stopped in his tracks when he saw me, not because my 200 pounds were of any threat to him, but no doubt because my symbolic uniform impressed him. At least for a second, anyway. Then in a rage similar to the one Hulk Hogan puts on, he ripped and stripped his T-shirt from his mammoth upper torso and flung it to the sidewalk. It was at that exact moment that I asked myself why I had been so hasty getting out of the safety of my police car—the one with the big push bumper on the front.

He was punctuating his incoherent shouts with that animalistic roar I had heard moments earlier and glaring at me with huge, wet eyes that seemed to have little bonfires in them. I told my portable radio to hurry my backup car and then tried to remember some of the de-escalation techniques I had learned in one of those touchy-feely classes I suffered through at in-service training. I started by asking him how he was feeling, to which he answered with that roar of his. Then he began moving toward me.

My brain kicked into Code-3 just as my cover car pulled up Code-2. I was happy to see that it was Irish, a big, blustery Irish officer who had worked the mean streets all of his career. He pulled around my car and parked in front of it, also having to park halfway into the lane. I looked back at the wrestler who had stopped for a moment, and I said something, hoping to stall him for a moment until Irish joined me on the sidewalk. He cocked his head like a dog trying to understand, then resumed his bear-like walk toward me. Just as I was wondering what it would feel like to have my arm eaten, there came a God-awful crash from the street.

I jerked my head toward Irish's car and saw his door bouncing 30 mph up the street in front of a city bus. For a second I didn't see Irish and just knew that the big cop was entangled around the bus's axle. Then I saw him through the police car's back window, still sitting behind his wheel and watching his car door journey up the street about 50 yards.

VIOLENCE

I dashed to the curb but I couldn't step into the street because several cars were screeching behind the bus that was also screeching to a stop. "Irish, you OK?" I shouted through the car window. He didn't answer so I yelled again. I just knew his leg was gone.

"Holy shit!" is all I heard over the traffic noise.

"Is he all right, Officer?" Bruno asked.

"I'm not sure," I answered. "Irish, you OK?"

"Holy shit! Yeah, I guess so," he called back. "I was just about to put my leg out when that bus hit my door. Holy shit!"

I exhaled a breath of relief, though probably not as big as the one Irish was exhaling.

"Damn, that was close, huh Officer?" Bruno asked.

"Yes it was," I said. Then it dawned on me that I was talking to Bruno. I turned slowly toward him. He was standing next to me, leaning out from the curb trying to hear and see Irish just as I was. We were like a couple of concerned buddies.

Bruno laughed. "Man, did you see that bus hit that cop car door? Wow, it just went bouncing up the street." He was suddenly as calm and gentle as a pussycat, now more concerned about Irish than he was about whatever had enraged him.

Irish scurried back to us at the curb. "You OK, here?" he asked, his usual red face even more red. I said I was and Bruno said he was, too.

"Good," he said, "'cause I gotta really go to the bathroom."

Bruno promised me he was not mad anymore and gave me his ID. I checked him for warrants and then checked with the bartender, who said Bruno could come back in if he behaved himself.

With Bruno's situation settled, I directed traffic around the bus and the police cars, while the bus driver and Irish (after using 555's rest room) filled out paperwork.

MY GLASSES

I started wearing glasses about halfway through my career. I didn't like it, but what are you going to do? My biggest concern was getting punched in the face and getting my black-framed specs driven into my handsome cheekbones. I was especially concerned about it, since I had once bloodied a guy's face doing that very thing in a high school brawl.

To be safe, I always put my glasses on the dash when I got out on a call. I would wear them as I raced through the streets to get there, but as I pulled to a stop, I automatically tossed them onto the dash no matter what the situation, since even a barking dog call can turn to crap in a quick second.

My partner and I were doing our usual 2 mph crawl along the busy skid row streets, checking out all the inhabitants and their activity. The sidewalks were so crowded that a drunk couldn't fall if he tried. We pulled to the curb in front of a mission and looked across the street, where several men were gathered around a used clothing store.

It was just a hole-in-the-wall place, big enough to set up a couple of long tables and lay out a few dozen shoes, coats, gloves, pants, and shirts. Some of the items were even washed, though most weren't. A few things were taken in trade, some were bought for 10 cents on the dollar, and other items were acquired at midnight when the owners were sleeping off their daily drunks in doorways.

We mentally dismissed the crowd as just a bunch of guys socializing and scooted ourselves low into our seats with the sole intention of doing no more than watching the passersby. A minute later a shout came from across the street. "Officers! Stop that man."

A man carrying a pair of boots burst through the crowd and bolted across the street toward us, zig-zagging around a couple of screeching cars. About 15 feet from us, he realized he was running directly toward the police. "Whoa!" he said. He made a hard right turn and charged up the street, then onto the sidewalk.

A guy we knew as the owner of the clothing store ran toward us.

"Officers! That man just ripped off a pair of boots from my shop."

My partner and I didn't need to say a word. I tossed my glasses on the dash and we both bailed out our doors. Like a couple of gazelles, we sprinted after the boot thief down the sidewalk, around the corner, and into a doorway where, to the man's chagrin, the door was locked. He fought a little but quit when we made him kiss the concrete.

Although we got a few cat calls, we were mostly cheered as we walked him back to the used clothing store. The shopkeeper was thankful, but said he didn't want to press charges since the guy was just another down-and-outer in need of a pair of boots. We gave the boots back to the shopkeeper, removed the handcuffs from the thief, and sent him on his way.

My partner was more angry than I was about the shopkeeper not pressing charges after we had gotten ourselves all sweaty and out of breath. "Hey, that's just the way it is on the row," I said. My comment didn't help and he continued with his grump as we walked across the street to our car.

"Hey, where are my glasses?" I said as we sat down. I looked all around the seat and on the floor. In our haste to leave, we hadn't locked the doors and my window was down. "Somebody swiped my glasses. One of these guys stole my glasses."

The dozen winos who had been leaning against the wall by our car were now gone. There were clusters of men at both ends of the sidewalk, but not a soul within 50 feet.

This cheered up my partner. He chuckled as he said, "Hey, that's just the way it is on the row."

THE ARSONIST

Bill and Caron had been a couple for a few days, which is a fairly long relationship among winos. They were both in their late 20s, and both well into a life of wine, beer, and sleeping in doorways, or wherever they happen to fall into an alcohol-induced sleep. Since it was summer, they had been mostly sleeping it off in a three-block long park on the edge of skid row.

Lots of people slept there in the summer, sometimes a hundred or more, lying under gray Salvation Army blankets or inside filthy sleeping bags. They weren't supposed to, and since the nearby businesses complained, my partner and I would have to wade in there every day to get people up and moving. Sometimes we would cruise by the park in the morning and see movement under a blanket or inside a sleeping bag, which left no doubt in our minds that those folks underneath were making a baby, or playing at it.

Bill and Caron always shared a sleeping bag and cuddled as snug as two bugs in a rug. On the morning in question, Bill had arisen and gone to the brick rest room to relieve himself of cheap wine and mission food. Finished with his duty, he staggered back to their spot only to find Caron riding atop a bearded guy wearing a red flannel shirt, and nothing else. It was apparent to Bill that not only was Caron a willing participant, but she was enjoying herself as much as the bearded stranger.

Bill flashed red. But instead of confronting the pair with angry words, he decided to get a weapon and kill them. He spun on his heels and ran one block to a service station where he bought a gas can filled with super supreme. Armed with the new weapon, he ran back to the park and worked his way through the sleepers, only to find that Caron and her new lover were no longer on top doing the sleeping bag mambo. They were now inside, completely covered from head to toe, apparently sleeping off their exertion.

Just when Bill thought he was as mad and hurt as he could get, the thought of them all cuddling and comfy where he had been less than 15 minutes earlier sent him into a blind rage. He twisted off the gas cap, tipped it upside down and drenched the sleeping bag from one end to the other. He cast the can aside and plunged his hand into his pocket to retrieve a Bic lighter.

When Bill tossed the can, it landed on top of a couple of guys sleeping a few feet away. They awoke and looked to see what was going on and, not being brain damaged winos but just a couple of down-and-outers, they put two and two together: the gas can lying on their blankets, the heavy smell of gas, and a guy angrily flicking his Bic over a dripping wet sleeping bag.

The two guys scrambled to their feet and lunged toward Bill, who put up a heck of a fight because he wanted to seriously kill his two-timing ol' lady and the bearded stranger. It was at this moment when my partner and I rounded the corner and saw a fight going on in the park. We told radio, climbed out of our car, and zig-zagged between the sleepers.

After we got them separated, Bill was howling because his thumb was broken and lying in a way it shouldn't across the back of his hand. The two guys filled us in on what had happened. "I had to break the man's finger," one of them told us. "He kept trying to get his lighter to flame even when we were wrestling with him. Look at that sleeping bag; it's drenched with gasoline."

We handcuffed Bill, who kept wailing about his thumb and how he wanted to barbecue the bearded guy and his ol' lady. While we listened to Bill's tale, one of the Good Samaritans pulled back the head end of the sleeping bag.

"What the hell . . ." Bill exclaimed, looking down at what he thought was going to be the heads of Caron and the bearded guy, but was instead a very sleepy and drunk 60-year-old man. "Where's Caron?"

"Is this your sleeping bag or not?" I asked Bill, since we were surrounded by dozens of others.

"Yeah, it's mine. And that's my pack beside it. But where's Caron and that bearded mother fucker?"

"Then who are you?" I asked the guy in the sleeping bag.

The old guy struggled to awaken. "Name's Jacob, Al Jacob. I didn't mean nothin'. I was just passing by and saw an empty sleeping bag. Nobody around, so I thought I'd catch a few Zs. Didn't mean to cause no trouble. I wasn't going to steal nothin'."

"Hey man," one of the Good Samaritans said to Bill. "You nearly torched the wrong guy."

Bill's face was turning to chalk.

The old man in the sleeping bag looked at each of us in obvious confusion as he vigorously rubbed his nose. "Hey, you fellas smell gas?"

VAN GOGH

My partner, Leon, and I were on foot when dispatch reported an assault right around the corner.

We found the victim, a middle-aged man, rubbing his jaw and leaning against a car parked at the curb. He was wearing jean overalls and a hooded sweatshirt with the hood up. He was a longtime skid row regular whom we had helped before with his spousal fights.

"Fightin' with Gerdie again, Jack?" I asked.

He rubbed his chin tenderly and said, "Yeah, she whacked me pretty good this time. Jaw feels broken."

Jack had been with Gerdie for years, though I didn't know if they were married. They drank hard and would be lovey-dovey one day and fight like a cat and dog the next. When the fights got physical, it was always one-sided, with Gerdie kicking the stuffing out of Jack.

"What's she mad about this time?" Leon asked.

Jack shook his head that he didn't know, then grimaced from the pain the movement caused. "Who knows? Sometimes she gets mad. You guys know that."

I knew it. "Where's she now?"

Jack shrugged, then rubbed his jaw again. "Who knows? She took off that way just before you guys showed up."

Leon stepped close to Jack and eyed his face. "She got you in the jaw pretty good, huh? Where else she hit you?"

Jack touched his stomach. "She punched me here, too. And she kicked me in the shin a couple of times. She was sure pissed. But I don't want to press charges or nothin'."

"Gerdie hit you with anything, Jack?" I asked.

"No. She did have a knife, though. Swung it at me crazy like about four times or so. Came real close to my face, too."

Leon looked close at Jack's hood. "Pull your hood back," he said. "I see something that looks like blood."

"Well, my ear does hurt some," Jack said, reaching for his hood. "But I don't remember her hitting me there."

79

Leon was standing on Jack's left side, and I was on his right, so I didn't see what my partner saw when the hood came down.

Leon's face suddenly blanched. "Whoa! Your ear! It's . . . gone!"

"What?" I said stepping next to Leon. Sure enough, Jack's ear was gone, clean as a whistle. There was some blood where his ear used to be and a small trickle of it running down his neck and into his sweatshirt hood.

"She definitely got you with that knife, Jack," I said. "Didn't that hurt? Doesn't it hurt now?"

He touched the side of his head and his face flashed with recognition that he no longer had an ear. He staggered as if he were going to pass out. My partner told radio to send an ambulance, then walked over behind the car.

"Sit down here on the curb and wait for the ambulance, Jack," I said. "I just can't believe you didn't notice when she cut it off. It's gotta hurt."

Jack's face was ashen as he lowered himself to the sidewalk. "It does now, Officer. It truly does now."

"Over here," Leon called from where he was squatting behind the car. His voice sounded raspy, nauseated. "Under the car here . . . It's the ear . . . lying here as pretty as you please."

In the distance we could hear the ambulance's siren.

Leon looked as if he were going to lose his lunch as I squatted next to him. I don't know why the sight of the ear didn't bother me as much as it did Leon. I looked at the ear lying all by itself, pink and perfect. There was even a little tuft of hair growing out of it.

"What do you think, Pard?" I asked. "You think that ear has been listening to everything we've been saying?"

STOLEN WALLET

"This happened a few years ago when patrol units were still dispatched on minor theft calls," says Officer Adams, a 22-year veteran. "Today, with the high volume of priority calls, we have a telephone unit where injured officers are assigned to take minor calls, like theft, lost briefcases, minor vandalism, or any minor situation where there is no suspect information. They take about 35,000 calls a year, which frees up patrol units for heavier stuff.

"Anyway, it was about 4 A.M., and I got a call to this flophouse hotel on a stolen wallet; the complainant was meeting me in the lobby. He was a cowboy, complete with the jeans, boots, cowboy's shirt, and hat. I assumed he was a good guy because his cowboy's hat was white. I asked him what happened.

"'Lost my wallet,' he said.

"'Where did you lose it?'

"'Not sure,' he said.

"I guessed right away that he was one of those cowboys of few words. 'How did it happen?' I asked, and he told me the following story, of which I had to dig for every little bit. Here is the condensed version:

"'Met a couple guys in a bar and we are drinkin' pretty good. They say they need a bath but got no place to get one. I tell 'em I'm in town just for the night 'cause I got to see the Veteran's Administration tomorrow. I says they can come up, we can drink some more, and they can have a bath. So one guy, who says his name is Pollack, goes down the hall and takes a bath and me and the other guy stay and drink. Then Pollack comes back and he and I drink while the other dude goes down the hall for a bath. I reckon I drank too much, 'cause my ass passes out. When I wake up, Pollack is gone and so is my wallet.'

"I asked the cowboy when all this happened, and he said around 11 P.M.—five hours earlier. I asked why he thinks Pollack did it and not the other guy.

"'Because the other guy is still up there.'

81

"'Where?' I asked.

"'Upstairs,' he says.

"'In your room?'

"'No, in the bathroom.'

"'He's still in the bathroom? Still in the bathtub?'

"'Yes,' he says.

"'It's 4 A.M. now. He's been in there for five hours?'

"The cowboy nodded. 'Yup, I think he's dead, too. He didn't look too good when I looked in.'

"I had been talking to the guy for 20 minutes before he dropped that bit of information on me. I had him lead me up the stairs and down the hall to his room. I checked to make sure Pollack hadn't come back, then we went down the hall to the community bathroom. I could hear water running inside, and when I opened the door, a thick wall of steam poured out into the hall. Six or seven cockroaches scurried out the door into the relatively fresh air of the hall. I knew it was bad in there if even the cockroaches wanted out.

"I took a couple steps in, fanning my way through the fog, and looked into the dead eyes of a man who otherwise looked as if he was enjoying a leisurely bath. His arms were draped over each side of the old claw-footed tub, his legs were over the far end, and his head rested above the water at the other end. He was submerged from his chest to his mid thighs. The water was scalding hot, probably just a degree below boiling. It wasn't flooding over because it was trickling in at the same rate it was trickling out through those holes near the top of the tub. The parts of his body out of the water were pasty white; those under the water were purple-red.

"But it was his balls that were really weird. They were bright red, swollen to the size of cantaloupe melons and floating on top of the water. They reminded me of a big red bobber, like you use when you go deep-sea fishing. They were really weird.

"I saw blood coming from the back of his head, so I called the detectives and the photo guys. To make a long story short, it turns out the guy had a heart attack as he was getting into the water and had fallen back, cracking his head on the tub.

"While the detectives were interviewing the cowboy in his room,

I took the opportunity to look around. That's when I found it—his wallet. It was lying under the bed. It hadn't been stolen at all. The cowboy probably dropped it there when he was drinking and was too drunk to know it.

"You know, if he hadn't called the cops because he thought his wallet had been stolen, the guy in the tub would probably still be soaking away in that scalding water.

"No telling how big his balls would be by now."

THE BRIDGE

Like a lot of redheads, Red has an explosive temper. He is a big man with a tight face, thick shoulders and chest, and arms forged from farm work and weightlifting. He is retired now, but when he worked the row he was like a lot of cops who worked the place: he was protective of the regular people who lived there, especially some of the winos who were so far out of it that they were easy prey to street predators.

"There is one thing that really pissed me off: jackrollers," Red says.

These were the assholes who showed up on the streets at the beginning of the month and again around the 15th—dates the guys got their social security checks, veteran checks, and other government money they were allotted. (Of course, most of the guys drank it up the first couple of days, then they would be broke until the next check.)

"Jackrollers came down to the row to rob the winos for their money, because they knew when the guys were staggering down a dark alley or lying on the sidewalk that they were easy, defenseless. Sometimes their money was just wadded up in their pockets, even hanging out. The jackrollers would either pull it out when the guy was passed out, or hit him over the head with something, or rib kick him unconscious. To me, jackrollers were the lowest form of animal. I loved to arrest them.

"One time, I had had it with a particularly slimy jackroller named Tuggs. I'd arrested him I don't know how many times, but he was always released and out walking around and jackrolling the next day. He was really violent and had hurt a lot of people over the past several months. It was the first of the month, so I had been keeping an eye out for him all night.

"Late into the shift, I rounded the corner on Miller Street and spotted Tuggs bent over a guy I knew as Old Ben. Ben was out like a light, and the jackroller was going through his pants pockets. I just flashed, seriously pissed. Tuggs saw me and tried to run, but I blocked his path with my car, jumped out, and grabbed him by his shoulders. He struggled a little, but fighting the cops wasn't his thing; he only picked on those who couldn't fight back. I searched him and tossed his ass in the backseat without handcuffing him. He was shouting and cursing, but I just ignored him and drove off—not toward the jail, though; I had another plan.

"It was a cold winter night with a heavy fog and practically nonexistent traffic. As soon as I turned to go up on the bridge, Tuggs quieted, having figured out that something was up. I stopped at mid span and sat there for a moment to see if any cars were going to pass. There wasn't a one. I guess only cops and jackrollers were out in the pea soup.

"I got out and jerked the back door open and told Tuggs to step out. He slid to the edge of the seat, his eyes really big, scared. 'What are you going to do?' he asked me in a little kid's voice. I grabbed him by his upper arms and jerked him out in one clean move, then ran him over to the cement railing and draped him halfway over it.

"'You going to keep ripping off my people?' I asked, trying to make my voice sound chilling.

"'Fuck you, Red!' he screamed. 'You can't do anything to me.'

"He was half right. The justice system sucked, and he knew and I knew that it was just a game. But my skid row people were still getting hurt by his kind. If the judges weren't doing anything to stop Tuggs, then I would do what I could. It was my responsibility as a peace officer.

"Tuggs screamed at me again and started to push back away from the railing. 'You can't—'

"But I didn't give him a chance to finish. I grabbed his ankles, jerked him off his feet, and lifted him over the edge. The fog was so thick that I couldn't see the water, which was churning about 50 feet below us. Tuggs couldn't see it either, but he definitely knew it was somewhere there in the black because he was screaming like a butchered pig. I was holding him by his ankles and he was making swimming motions in the air with his arms. He didn't kick around, though, because he didn't really want me to let go.

"'You going to rip off my people, anymore?' I shouted.

"'Ohshitohshitohshit!' is all I got out of him. My arms were getting tired, but I was so pissed that all I could think about was scaring him so he would stop stealing from my boys.

"'Are you, dammit?' I was definitely beginning to feel the strain of his weight. 'Are you going to keep—' One of his shoes popped off, making me lose hold of one ankle.

"His screams were deafening and he was wiggling like a worm on a hook. 'Stop moving,' I shouted at him. I was trying to grab his one ankle with my other hand, but instead I grabbed his shoe, and it came off just like the other one. That startled him and me, and he twisted just enough that he broke loose from my grip.

"I still remember how he looked up at me, his arms flailing and his legs sort of running in the air as he dropped head first out of sight into the dense fog.

"I screamed something; I don't remember what. Time froze, and then what seemed like several seconds later, I heard a splash from way down below.

"I panicked. 'Oh man,' I was thinking, 'I just killed the fucker!' I looked around to see if anyone saw me, but there wasn't a person or a car in sight. Everything was painted in a weird orangish light from the fog-covered street lamps on the bridge. I jumped in my police car, cranked a U-turn and raced down the bridge and through the barren streets to a place where I could get close to the water. I raced along the roadway that parallels the river bank until I was under the bridge. I shined my spotlight into the water, but the fog prevented the light from going past the embankment. I called out Tugg's name a couple of times, but stopped because I knew someone might hear me and be a witness later.

"I must have walked back and forth on that embankment for an hour, but I never saw or heard Tuggs. I looked until the end of my shift, then went back to the station. I didn't tell anyone and I didn't know what to do. I definitely didn't sleep that night.

"The next day I came in early and went through the reports to see if Tuggs had been found in the river. Nothing. I casually asked a few skid row officers and some of the street people if they had seen Tuggs. No one had.

"Then, about three days later, I was taking a theft report from a guy on the corner, when Tuggs walked around the building and practically bumped into me. He froze and I froze. Finally, I got my heart out of my mouth and coughed out, 'Tuggs!' That's all it took. He spun around about the fastest I have ever seen a human move and was gone in a flash.

"I never saw him after that and the jackrolling statistics dropped to about half of what they had been. One thing is for sure: I never did the bridge trick on anyone else."

ROLL PLAYING

Whenever jackrolling reached epidemic proportions, we would send an officer into skid row to play the role of a passed-out drunk. The officer would dress in his oldest, most tattered clothes, rub some grime into his exposed skin, allow a bottle of wine to protrude from his jacket pocket, and then find a doorway to lie in. Though the liberals cried entrapment, he would place a wad of paper money in his pocket so that the bills hung out in plain sight.

One time I went to shake a sleeper awake and he grabbed my ankle. Not waiting to find out what he had in mind, I smacked him in the forehead with my palm. "Ouch!" the guy yelled. "Take it easy, Christensen. I'm just jerkin' you around." The "wino" was really Dave Barker, an officer dressed up and made up to look like a down-and-outer. I hadn't been told there was an undercover jackroller mission going on in my district.

"Whoops, sorry," I said. But Dave remained pissed. Oh well, he shouldn't have grabbed my ankle.

On another occasion we conducted a mission and the suspect turned out to be one of the Greek store owners in the area. He not only had our marked bait money on him, but thousands of other dollars that he had been taking from passed out drunks on his street. The Greek community was outraged and embarrassed by the guy and forced him to plead guilty.

Some jackrolling missions were so productive that we couldn't keep up with the paperwork. We would make more arrests than we had cops to write the reports and haul the thieves to jail. "Seize the opportunity" seemed to be the operative phrase of the day among the jackrollers on the row.

Jones, or Jonesy as everyone calls him, who still works the area today, told me of a time when he worked a jackrolling mission. "Several years ago they had me playing a passed-out wino in a doorway. The jackrollers were really hitting the area, and some of the drunks were getting beaten up badly. Some had even been stabbed for the few dollars they had left after their drinking bout.

VIOLENCE

"I was dressed for the part and had been given $200 in bait money, which I slipped halfway into my shirt between the buttons," says Jones. "It was about 11 P.M. when I sprawled out in a filthy doorway with a bottle of Mad Dog 20/20 in my hand. My cover officers were across the street, sitting low in an unmarked car.

"It didn't take long for a jackroller to spot me, the 'helpless victim.' The guy stepped quickly into the doorway and looked both ways down the sidewalk. The streetlight was broken out, so that section of the block was in deep shadows; my doorway was even darker. But there was a patch of light from somewhere falling across me, enough that the jackroller could see what he wanted to take—my damn watch.

"Like most guys working skid row, I wear only a $25 watch to work, since we get in a lot of fights down here and the bands are always quick to break. The bureau only reimburses us for $25 on a lost or broken one. I guess the guy only saw my watch, so that's what he took. He just stripped it right off my wrist and then tore off down the street.

"He only got a half block before the two backup guys had him in custody. Normally that would be the end of the story: the suspect gets arrested, taken to the station, the reports are written, we ridicule him for missing the cash, then we take him to booking. But there is one more aspect to this case.

"'Hey,' I asked. 'Has anyone searched the jackroller?' I was busy writing my report and just assumed the other guys searched him. But something told me to ask, anyway.

"'I didn't,' one of the backup officers said. 'I just stuffed him in the holding room. I think my pard did.'

"'Nope,' the other officer says. 'I thought you did.'

By now, we were all moving toward the holding room. I peeked through the keyhole and saw that the jackroller was sitting on the bench with his hands still cuffed behind him. We all went in and I started searching the guy.

"I found a gun in his waistband. It looked like an old .32 revolver.

"'Shit!' one of the guys said. We were all upset at how we had screwed up.

"Then I looked at the gun closer. 'Wait a minute,' I said. 'This is a starter pistol.'

"'It is?' the jackroller asks, surprised. 'That son-of-a-bitch who sold it to me said it was real.'

"I laughed at the guy. 'Well, sucker. You got taken.'

"The jackroller was really mad. 'I even put real bullets in it,' he said.

"'You what?' one of the other guys, who's a range officer, said. I handed him the gun.

"'You sure the hell did,' he said, tapping out .22 long rifle cartridges. 'If you had fired this, you just might have lost your pinkies, pal.'

"'Damn,' the jackroller said, looking real dejectedly at the floor. 'I can't do nothin' right.'

"'Not true, my friend,' I said to him. 'You picked a good night to go to jail. It's starting to rain out there.'"

TIME FOR A VACATION

Day after day after stinking day working skid row takes its toll
even on those cops whose senses are dulled and no longer seem
affected by anything they see. But the sights and sounds of the place
do have a cumulative effect, so in order to keep working there (why
that should be a goal is an issue that should be taken up with a
shrink), it's essential from time to time to get away from the place.

I have trained and taught the martial arts since 1965, and I travel frequently to San Francisco to train with friends and instructors
there. Some people like to lie in the sun on a deck overlooking a lake
and nap their tensions away. I like to kick people in the chest and get
thrown on thin jujitsu mats. It makes me feel better.

For just a few months, there was a small travel agency right
smack in the middle of the action on the row. The company was new
and most likely didn't have a lot of working capital, so setting up an
office in a low-rent area probably seemed like a good idea to them.
No doubt their naiveté vanished quickly.

One day I had had it up to here with skid row; I needed desperately to get out of Dodge (or Portland, as was the case). So I
stopped by the travel agency to check on flight times and dates. They
had cozied up the place nicely, and it really did look like a travel
agency. There were three desks, posters of far-off places on the walls,
a nice carpet on the floor, a few ferns, and pretty Hawaiian music on
the stereo. But just outside the big plate-glass window was a whole
other world that was scaring the poop out of the two middle-aged
women working there. The shop had been open for only a couple
weeks, and they had already seen more out those windows than
most people see in a lifetime.

"Come in, Officer," they said in unison, practically shouting at
me. "Can we get you some coffee? Cookies? Sit down, please."

I did a little small talk, and then told them I was interested in
getting a ticket to San Francisco. They were more than attentive, and
I caught on quickly that they were trying to keep me in the place.
Several times they mentioned for me to tell other officers that they

91

could stop in any time they wanted and have a cup of coffee and a cookie. They asked me a lot of questions about skid row, and I gave them several safety tips and told them how to call us if they needed the police in a quick second. I just started to tell them how I was in desperate need of a break from the place, when the face of the woman I was sitting across from turned white. "Oh my God," she cried out, pointing past me out the window. "Look at what's going on over there."

I twisted in the chair and looked beyond the hanging fern. Across the street, a 20-something street person armed with a broken bottle was slashing at an old wino. I sprang out of the chair and was out the door, pulling my stick from its holder as I crossed the street.

A word about my stick. I practice three martial arts: karate, jujitsu, and arnis, the latter a Filipino fighting art that uses, among other weapons, a 24-inch-long rattan stick. The rattan is hard, difficult to break, and weighs about six ounces, compared to 22 ounces that some police batons weigh. Its light weight makes the delivery of the somewhat exotic techniques extremely fast.

I yelled at the armed guy who now had the helpless wino cringing against a wall. When he turned to face me, I saw that he was holding a wine bottle in each hand, one bottle broken with jagged, protruding shards, the other unbroken. He took a step forward, his face blank and hard to read as to his intentions. I ordered him to drop the bottles, but he just stood there. I advanced slowly, telling him one more time to drop the bottles. He didn't. So I made my move.

In arnis, the movement *abaniko* means "the fan." Actually, the movement is more like the swiping motion of a windshield wiper, a technique that can be executed fast due the light weight of the weapon.

I hit him with abaniko. The fast swipe to my left struck his right wrist, and the swipe to the right hit his left. The pain from the first blow made him cry out and release the whole bottle. My second blow landed on his other hand before the first bottle hit the cement, and he cried out again, the struck nerves causing his hand to pop open and release the broken bottle. Several street people standing near cheered and gave me a round of applause.

I cuffed him, shoved him into the back of my police car, and then got the wino's name and story before I sent him on his way. After I made sure my car was locked, I went back into the travel agency, since it was just a few minutes before the end of my shift, and I needed to get the tickets.

"So," I said to the two white-faced, gaping-mouthed women. "What flights you got for next Friday?"

PART THREE

BODILY EXCRETIONS

The subject of bodily excretions is

not discussed in polite society. Most of your friends and acquaintances don't want to know about your bowel movements—especially when they are of the dysentery variety—and they don't want to hear you discuss your last vomiting experience, or witness you vomiting, for that matter. People are a little more liberal when it comes to the subject of peeing, though most wouldn't want to see you do it, or stand in the way when you do it. Most people don't want to see blood, especially when there is a lot of it and double especially when it's their own. And mucous, a.k.a. snot, is undoubtedly the number-one secretion that is loathed universally.

Probably one of the many reasons skid row is avoided by so many people is that more bodily excretions are seen there than anywhere else, except maybe on a baby's changing table. There were times when I would wrestle a wino to his feet—who would have a snot bubble the size of a tennis ball, a dinner-plate-sized urine stain on the front of his pants, and an even larger wine-shit stain on the back—just as a straight citizen would walk by, giving us a startled look. I was so used to seeing all this that I no longer saw it for the loathsomeness that it was until I viewed it through a straight person's shocked eyes. Then I, too, would be disgusted—and wonder what was happening to me that I was no longer affected by the scummy world in which I spent my days.

While I always made an effort to treat all of skid row's inhabitants with respect and dignity, sometimes it was a real effort, especially when a guy or gal was covered from head to toe with slime of every bodily excretion possible.

Here are a few stories that help paint a picture of bodily functions gone awry. Don't read this section if you have eaten recently. You've been warned.

BODILY EXCRETIONS

WINE SHITS

Wine shits on skid row are as plentiful as flies, in fact, the two go together. If you have celebrated too hard the night before, you know what wine shits are like the day after. They are miserable, they hurt, and the stench is horrific. If there is anything positive about the experience, it's that you have a nice bathroom to go to. Winos don't. They go in their clothes, over and over again. Sometimes wine shits were like a plague on skid row: everyone we took to the detoxification center had them. We always carried a can of air freshener (the pine forest scent works best) in the glove box, but there were some guys, even with all the windows down and with repeated sprays, who could still gag a maggot.

When I joined the PD in the '70s, the backseats were covered with porous vinyl, and we could take the seat out at the police garage and hose it down, then put it back in. This removed the slime, but after 50 washes, the odor stayed in the vinyl and we had to work the eight hours breathing it in. Keeping the windows rolled down helped a little, but that got cold in the winters.

Years later, the seats were benches made of solid plastic, which made it hard to wash the big messes out. The smaller ones could be sprayed with a cleaner at the garage and wiped down with paper towels. But if the wino was especially bad, and his wine shits ran down his leg onto the floor, we would return the car to the basement and write up a request form to have the car detailed. If all the cars were on the road, however, we were stuck for the balance of the shift.

Some of us got used to the smell, while the more sensitive complained the entire shift. For the calloused, it would take a ride-along, such as a college student, a foreign visitor, or an interested citizen, to remind us of how the car stunk.

"Oh my God!" they would say. "What is that horrible smell? It smells like . . ."

"Yes, it is," I'd say. "And, by the way, welcome to skid row."

IT'S ALL GOOD

Death is as common as cockroaches in skid row flophouses and cheap hotels that offer rooms for a buck or two a night. When the desk clerk hasn't seen a "guest" for a few days, he either checks the room himself with a pass key, or gives the police a call. The clerk will usually tell the officers that he doesn't feel right about entering the room, though he has every right to do so. The truth is that some clerks are apprehensive about checking on "one not seen" for fear of what they will find behind the locked door.

The desk clerk at the Homer Hotel called 911 and told the operator that there were a man and woman in 204 who hadn't been seen for at least a week. "Maybe they kilts one another," the toothless old-timer told the operator. "There's a terrible smell a comin' from the crack at the bottom of the door, and I just becha they's dead inside."

"OK," the operator said. "Just hang on and there will be an officer there shortly."

Warren Koenig was a salty skid row cop who had seen just about everything there was to see as a cop, and especially one working on the row. He and his partner, Anderson, walked up to the counterman and nodded a greeting. "What you got, Ed?" Koenig asked around the stub of his cigar.

"Got a couple of old drinkers up in 204. Haven't seen them fer a while and there's startin' to be a pretty good damn stink comin' out of theres."

"Who are they?" Koenig asked, turning the ledger around. He ran his finger down the rows until he found 204. "Wilma Thompson and Billy Thompson. Yeah, we know them. A couple of hard-drinking winos."

"It's been a week since you've seen them?" Anderson asked.

Ed nodded vigorously. "At least, Officers. At least that long."

"OK, give me the key," Koenig said, relighting his cigar. "We'll take a look."

The officers climbed the stairs to the second floor. "I hate these

BODILY EXCRETIONS

calls," Anderson said as they stopped before 204. "Oh, man. What a smell!"

Koenig shrugged as if he could care less and inserted the key. He pushed the door open and was greeted by a wave of stench that literally knocked the officers back a step. "Holy shit!" Anderson cried, spinning around and gagging violently, nearly losing the greasy-spoon breakfast he had eaten earlier.

The room was roughly 15 by 15 feet with a bed, broken nightstand, and wooden chair. The air was thick with cigarette smoke, and the once-white walls were yellow with it. The one window was so filmed over with smoke and cooking grease that it was impossible to see out; it allowed only a diffused, gray light into the room. The floor was carpeted with empty wine bottles, cigarette butts, empty food cans, wrappers, and vomit and wine-shit splatters, old and fresh.

The bed, a long-broken-down mattress on a broken bed frame, was a tangle of filthy, tattered blankets and sheets. All were covered with wine shit, wet and dried. It covered the blankets, the sheets, the pillows, and it had run down the sides of the mattress. The air over the bed literally swam from the thick smell.

The couple were lying side-by-side in the bed, spooning.

Koenig stepped into the room; Anderson stayed in the hall, asking, "Foul play?" He assumed they were dead. He burst forth with another round of gagging coughs.

"They are foul, all right," Koenig said around puffs from his stogie. "But they're alive as hell."

"What the—" an unshaven, heavy-lidded face looked up over a wad of brown-smeared blanket. "Officer Koenig," Billy slurred. "What the hell's going on?"

Wilma's head appeared next, just long enough for Koenig to see what her hair was matted with. She moaned and her head plopped back down.

The two had been on a drinking binge for several days, spending most—if not all—of it in bed, too out of it to even stagger down the hall to the bathroom. The woman was in especially bad shape,

99

SKID ROW
B E A T

passing in and out of consciousness several times. They ordered an ambulance for her.

While Anderson stayed in the hall, under the pretense of directing the ambulance crew to the room, Koenig stepped over to the side of the sewage bed. He looked over the mess, squinted through his cigar smoke, then asked in his usual straightforward manner, "So tell me, Billy, is she a good piece of ass?"

The old wino struggled up on one elbow, indifferent to the brown smears on his bare chest and shoulders. His crusted lips spread in a rotten-tooth smile. "It's all good, officer. Some's better than others, but it's all good."

100

BODILY EXCRETIONS

A GOOD DEFENSE

"I was cruising through a parking lot one Sunday morning," says Officer Kramer, "doing a little public relations waving and nodding to the nicely dressed people who parked there, then walked to one of the downtown churches. It was a beautiful, sunny morning, and the many families unloading from station wagons and vans seemed happy in the spring warmth that bathed the city.

"At least they were until they noticed the squatting, grizzled wino a few feet away, his filthy drawers pulled down, as he sprayed wine-laced diarrhea onto the asphalt.

"First I saw the shocked look on the churchgoers' faces, then I looked to where they were looking. I goosed my car over there and parked so at least some of the people couldn't see him. Before I could say anything to the guy, he groaned, 'It's hell when you got the wine shits, Officer.'

"'Well, that may be true, but it's against the law to do that in public,' I said. I told him to pull up his pants and put his hands behind his back. He was madder than a wet hornet because I was arresting him. 'It's hell when you got the wine shits,' he said again. 'Don't you understand that, Officer?' I told him once again that, nonetheless, he couldn't void them out there in the middle of a public parking lot in front of nice families.

"This just made him madder. 'The hell with those people,' he said from my backseat. He was glaring out the window at them. 'They don't know what it's like to have the wine shits. They just don't understand.'

"I transported the guy back to the station, wrote him a disorderly conduct citation, then let him go. I wrote up the report, noting exactly what the wino had said repeatedly about his condition. A few days later I got the usual form letter from a deputy district attorney, saying that he agreed with my arrest and had issued a formal complaint charging the wino.

"But the DA must have had some empathy with the wino's condition because on the bottom of the note he had jotted in longhand, 'But we must be cautious of the "wine shits" defense.'"

WHITE STUFF

"When I reached for his wine bottle," Officer Roberts says, "the guy jerked his hand away and it looked for a second as if he were going to hit me with it. He was a scroungy old black man, wrinkled and shriveled up, without a tooth in his face. He had shoots of long whiskers around his mouth like an alley cat.

"I sidestepped and grabbed his free arm and spun him around so that he couldn't clobber me with that bottle. He spat out a string of cuss words and struggled for his footing as he tried to strike at me. I had no choice but to dump him onto his old butt.

"He landed a little harder than I had intended, and sort of coughed out an 'oomph' sound. He dropped the wine bottle, and it rolled across the sidewalk and into the gutter. I reached for my cuffs, but then he started to fight me again. He swung his fists at my legs and scooted toward me like a land crab. I circled around behind him and pulled his shoulders down so that he plopped onto his back. I grabbed both his wrists and began dragging him toward my car. He squirmed and kicked at the air, but I managed to drag him a few feet.

"Then I noticed the white stuff.

"It was coming out of the bottom of his right pant leg, which was bunched up around his upper calf from all the thrashing about. The white stuff oozed down over his shin, over his ragged sock, then over his battered, dirty old sneaker.

"It was sort of a stream, like toothpaste, but not quite as pasty. He looked down at it, too, and stopped fighting me. He didn't say anything, but I could tell he was scared, though he didn't act like he was hurt. It was oozing onto the sidewalk now, and I was beginning to think about calling an ambulance. I had taken him down harder than I had meant to, and I was thinking that he probably busted an intestine, or somehow jarred loose his entrails. I just knew it was coming out of his butt.

"I rolled him onto his stomach so I could examine his backside. I noticed that his OD-colored military pants were two sizes too big for him and that the seat had old wine-poop stains. I was about to

102

pull his pants down to check him out to see where the white stuff was coming from, when I noticed the wetness around the big pocket on his upper thigh.

"'What you got in there?' I asked.

"'Mazenuh,' he said, or something like that. He was really drunk and hard to understand. Now the white stuff was all over the ground by his foot, which he was scooting around in it.

"'What?' I asked him.

"'Maz naze,' he said.

"'Are you saying mayonnaise?'

"'Yes, muthafucker,' he said. 'Maz naze. You broke the jar I keeps in my pocket.'"

THEY'RE IN THE TRUNK

Richard was one of the most muscular police officers I had ever seen. He had muscles in places where average people don't even bathe. His face looked as if it had been chiseled from stone, complete with a thick blood vein that trailed down his forehead and disappeared into an eyebrow. The vein bulged and throbbed whenever he got pissed, though he was usually an even-tempered officer. But after a while, skid row could even test the patience of Mother Theresa.

He had worked in the row for 10 years, usually in the paddy wagon, scooping up a dozen or more drunks at a time and driving them to the detoxification center. He had seen every kind of degradation man can sink to, and he usually handled his calls with patience and professionalism. However, there were times when all that, and his compassion, went out the window.

The paddy wagon was broken down one night and his partner had called in sick, so Richard signed out a car and went out alone. He was starving and wanted to hit one of the Chinese joints right away for some stir-fried vegetables. Dispatch got to him first, though, giving him a call on three passed-out winos in the doorway of a long-closed movie theater. The veggies would have to wait.

Richard was going to ask for backup, but when he arrived at the call, all three winos were in a deep, wine-induced slumber. He decided to handle it himself. Usually, when he was alone and got a call on three winos, he would stuff one or two in the backseat, run them to the detox center, then come back and get the remaining one or two. This was the safest way to transport them, since it was common for winos to fight in the backseat, motivated as they were by alcohol, cramped conditions, and anger over going to the detox.

Richard twisted the ear of the closest man, who awoke with a sputter. "Come on. Get on your feet, pardner," Richard said, lifting him by his arms. Then, "What the—" Richard backed away from the man who slumped against the old theater door. The entire seat of the wino's pants was soaked in liquid feces. Richard shook his head with disgust and decided to put the guy on hold for a second.

BODILY EXCRETIONS

He squatted next to the second wino, noticing immediately that the man's tattered jacket sleeve was soaked from where the first man had been lying against him. Then he saw that the man's trousers were also soaked from his own wine shits.

That was enough to negate all of Richard's usual compassion. His 10 years of working skid row, his hunger for Chinese food (though the scene before him had momentarily killed his appetite), and now two guys with wine shits were all that he could take.

"There is no way any of you are going to stink up my car," he said angrily to the two guys who were oblivious in their drunken stupors, and to the third who was still passed out. "You're all riding in the back. The very back."

He inserted his key into the trunk lock, popping the lid open. He pushed a box of report forms to the side and tossed the first-aid kit back as far it would go. He took two strides over and grabbed the first wino, who had nearly slid all the way down the wall, and pulled him over to the trunk. Richard put one hand behind his head and jammed the man headfirst inside, where he lay without complaint, snoring happily by the time Richard grabbed the second guy. He resisted a little, but Richard's strength was too much for him. A moment later he was dropped into the trunk on top of the first guy. He tried to get up, but Richard's menacing voice, not to mention the site of that throbbing forehead vein, was just too intimidating. The first guy in the trunk continued to snore in spite of his heavy blanket.

"Come on," Richard commanded the third man. He jerked the drunk to his feet and walked him three steps toward the trunk before the man awoke.

"What the—" is all the drunk got out as Richard picked him up like a toddler and dropped him unceremoniously into the trunk on top of the second guy. Richard then pushed him off the pile, stuffing him behind the first two and next to the spare tire. He lowered the trunk slowly to ensure he didn't pinch anyone or anything. It shut snugly.

"Got to appreciate these big Ford trunks," he said to himself as he slid in behind the steering wheel.

Richard would have gotten away with this little violation of the

105

rules if it hadn't been for one of the bleeding-heart workers at the detox center seeing him removing his human cargo.

In the ensuing investigation, the brass didn't care that he had been cranky and that the winos smelled at their worst. There may not have been a written rule about hauling people in the trunk of police cars, but it nonetheless was in bad taste and not sensitive to those afflicted with alcoholism.

Richard lost 30 days' pay; he also became a legend on the bureau.

BODILY EXCRETIONS

THE BRICK SHIT HOUSE

There is a park of sorts on the edge of skid row with a brick rest room in its middle. The park takes up about one third of a city block and was probably part of a much larger park a few dozen decades ago, but was somehow left out as buildings and streets grew around it. It's too small now to do anything with, so it has remained a dinky little grassy area with a couple of big fir trees that provide shade for the locals.

The old unisex rest room sits under the trees like a dinosaur and, as one would imagine a dinosaur to be, it has been a long-time annoyance to the police. We asked the city to close it years ago because it served only as a shooting gallery for the hypodermic crowd and as a crash pad for winos. There were too many people getting hurt and dying inside the place, so we thought it best to get the door sealed. Amazingly, the city took our advice and shut it down, but the door never stayed sealed for long.

Once every two or three weeks, we would check the rest room and find the door kicked in and one or two people sleeping on the floor inside. We would shoo them out and call for a city maintenance crew to once again bolt the door shut.

The rest room was about 15 feet by 20, with four old toilets that had long ago lost their seats. There were no stalls; those too had long ago been removed. There were just toilets, a couple of sinks, and a vile, foul odor that would never ever be removed.

It had been ice-raining for a couple days and my partner and I had been too busy with traffic problems to check on the place, so when we finally did, we were not surprised to find the door forced open. There were a half dozen backpacks outside the door under some overgrown shrubbery, which indicated there were at least six people inside, probably more. There were more.

The smell that gushed out the door literally staggered us back a step. We were familiar with the old stench, one that had accumulated from years of use and had permeated the dank, brick walls. While the old odor was still present, it had been reduced to just an under-

107

current, overpowered now by a fresh, thicker stench. When we pulled open the door, it roared through the opening, similar to what happens when a hole tears into the side of an aircraft. What we wouldn't have given for those little orange oxygen masks to have dropped down from the ceiling.

Although our eyes were watering intensely, we counted 14 men and women in the dark dankness. There were three in a corner who were swapping swigs from a gallon wine jug, one man was urinating into one of the overflowing toilets, and two others, a man and a woman, were sitting on the seatless toilets, adding to the overflow. The floor was slimy with waste water, though ignored by all who slept in their bedrolls, even the guy who was curled around the unoccupied toilet sleeping like a child.

"Good morning everyone," I said. "There is quite a crowd in here this morning."

"Damn cold out there," the 50-something woman said from where she was straining on the toilet. Her breath fogged around her mouth.

"Not too cozy in here either," my partner said, looking at the bottom of his shoe. He normally worked a nicer part of town where there were no winos and no problem public rest rooms. He was forced to work skid row on this day because we were short of people, an assignment he hadn't taken well and had been complaining about all morning.

"How long you been here?" I asked the woman, as I stepped a little closer to her throne.

"I've only been sitting here about 30 minutes, Officer."

"No, I mean how long have you been staying in this place?"

"Oh." She shrugged and strained a little. "Uh, let's see. A week maybe. Is it OK? I'm new in town."

"Well, normally the door is bolted shut, but someone must have kicked—"

"We didn't do it, Officer." She looked between her legs and checked something in the dirty water, then looked back up to me. "It was that way when we came in."

"Excuuuuse me!" my partner said into my ear. "May I interrupt this little coffee chat for a sec?" The sarcasm in his voice was as thick

BODILY EXCRETIONS

as the odor in the room. I looked at him as he continued in the same voice. "Do you realize you are talking to a woman who is taking a dump? The dump is happening in progress as you chat? You realize that, right?"

He had a point, though I felt he could have been a little nicer about making it. I guess I had just been working skid row too long to notice such things anymore.

"OK," I said. "Let's go. They can stay here. They're not hurting anyone."

"Thank you," he said, and bolted out the door.

BRAIN GOO

"A road crew picking up trash along I-405 has found a 55," the female dispatcher said. A 55 is police code for a dead body. "They're standing by waiting for you where Long Street crosses. The medical examiner has been notified."

I rogered the call and headed for the address. I was already feeling a little queasy, having just gotten over the flu, so I wasn't in the mood for anything icky, though dead body calls rarely bothered me, anyway.

The county clean-up crew had been picking up trash along a fence that bordered an embankment above the I-405 freeway. As I pulled to the curb, I noted about 10 of them leaning on their rakes and about a half dozen passersby gathered on the sidewalk. A supervisor wearing an orange vest and a hard hat greeted me and pointed down the 15-foot embankment. "The guy is down there, lying next to the fence. I'm no expert, officer, but he looks like he's been there a while. It scared the shit out of my worker, that black kid over there by the truck. He almost turned white scrambling up the embankment and screaming like crazy."

I started to laugh but managed to keep my demeanor. I side-stepped down the steep embankment and pushed aside the branches of an overgrown bush. The man, dressed in typical mission give-away clothes, was lying on his back, flush against the cyclone fence. Sixty feet farther down the embankment, freeway traffic roared by. Most of the flesh on the man's face, and the one hand that I could see, was rotted away, leaving almost a skeleton with patches of leathery skin and the occasional tuft of hair. His eyes were gone, exposing only empty sockets, and his lips were gone, too, giving him a toothy grimace straight out of hell. The supervisor was right: the guy had been lying in this place for a while.

I turned around to walk back up the embankment and nearly ran into a crowd of rubberneckers. I shooed them back up to the sidewalk because if I had a homicide, it was important to keep the area clean.

BODILY EXCRETIONS

A few minutes later, a white van pulled to the curb with the words "Medical Examiner" on its side. A young man, emanating enthusiasm, scrambled out of the driver's door and jogged around the front of the van and onto the sidewalk. The passenger's door swung open, and a character straight out of a Hollywood B-grade movie stepped out. He must have been 6 feet, 5 inches, at maybe 140 pounds if he was wearing a heavy coat. I guessed he was in his early 60s, pale as chalk, wearing a black suit with jacket sleeves far too short for his endlessly skinny arms. He told me later that he had been an ME for 40 years.

"What do you have?" the young pup asked eagerly.

"He's down there," I pointed. "You tell me what I got." Over the pup's shoulder the tall, pale man smiled at his young charge's energy.

I followed them down the embankment, ready to catch the old man if he took a tumble. I watched as the two poked around the deceased and listened to the old man's soft voice as he pointed out things to his young partner. After a few minutes, the old man straightened and cleared his throat. "Well, it looks like he's been here for about a year or so. Of course, we can give you a better time later. It's possible he's been here even longer, since he's been under these thick bushes and out of the elements. Sometimes decomposition slows when the body is out of the sun and rain. I don't see blood stains or anything to indicate foul play. Of course, we'll know more when we take a closer look at him back at the shop. Right now, I'm thinking he probably held up here to get out of the weather, then died in his sleep. He went undetected because he's down here out of sight."

I nodded. "OK, you going to take him now?"

The old man looked at the pup. "Get the bag, Larry."

I moved back up the embankment and told the crowd to stay on the sidewalk. The young ME retrieved the green bag then scooted back down the embankment. I told the workers and the growing crowd that the dead man was a natural so there wasn't anything to see.

That's when the old ME climbed up the embankment carrying the dead man's head.

"Dang if it didn't come right off," he said nonchalantly, turning it around in his hands as if examining a melon at the supermarket.

111

There was a collective gasp from the crowd, followed by an exodus as every last one of them scooted across the street to the other sidewalk. I was about to join them when the old ME continued. "Say, Officer, you want to know how to determine the sex by looking at the skull? See the thickness around the eye sockets . . ." He rattled on for a minute about how to tell the difference between a man and woman by looking at a rotting skull. Two days earlier, when my flu was at it's worst, I had been calling "Ralph!" into the toilet every hour. I could feel that familiar tingle again.

Then the head did something that made the feeling worsen.

All the jostling must have loosened something in the broken area where the head had been attached to the neck, because a stream of gray goo suddenly gushed out and splattered onto the sidewalk. "Whoa," the old ME said, as if he had done nothing more than slosh his cup of coffee. "Still got some fluid in it." Across the street the crowd moaned, and then began moving off in different directions.

I felt my face flush and prickly heat spread over my body. I turned quickly away and walked toward my car like I had a reason to do so. I occupied my mind with thoughts of mowing my lawn, playing catch with my dog, and sweeping my patio—anything to keep me from heaving all over the street.

Leaning against my car, I watched the MEs carry the body bag up the embankment and place it on a gurney they had parked on the sidewalk. I don't know what the old ME did with the head; I'm assuming he took it back down the embankment and added it to the body bag. They wheeled the gurney to the back of the van and loaded it in. Apparently, in a final inspection, the old man unzipped the bag and gave the deceased another look.

"Uh-oh, Larry," I heard him say in his soft, monotone voice, with his head practically inside the bag. "We're missing a hand. He's gotta have two."

"I'll have a looksee," Larry said enthusiastically, and took off once more down the embankment. The old man looked over at me and shook his head as if to say, "Kids nowadays."

I smiled back, fighting the rage that was happening in my stomach, my intestines, and my head.

112

BODILY **EXCRETIONS**

"Here it is, Paul," the young man called out as he scrambled up the embankment. "One hand coming up." Then in an "aren't we silly?" voice, "It was covered with leaves."

It was December and freezing outside, but I climbed into my car and turned the air conditioner on my face, full force.

FIGHTING IN THE JOHN

It was called Old Town Cafe, and it had been there forever. It defined the term "greasy spoon," and if you didn't mind getting your arteries clogged with paste-thick cholesterol, your lungs congested from the pea-soup fog of tobacco smoke, and your stomach lining destroyed from coffee so strong that a roach could skitter across it without sinking, then you would be in hog heaven there.

The booths were the rolled vinyl kind, bright red, with tears repaired by gray duct tape. The tables had seen as many drunken foreheads resting on their tops as they had beer glasses and steaming cups of thick, black coffee. A wall separated the restaurant from the bar, with common doorways at each end. The restaurant had its occasional problems—no-pays, sleeping drunks, fights—but the bar had problems every day, so much so that if we didn't wrestle a mean drunk out of there at least once a week, we felt slighted.

There were men's and women's rest rooms in the common doorway at the back of the restaurant. The women's was filthy; the men's was beyond filthy, so much so that the word "filthy" would be a compliment. The men's was roughly 6 feet by 12 feet with two urinals and two toilet stalls. More times than not, both urinals and both toilets were clogged and overflowing onto the cement floor, making the air so thick it would dull a hacking machete. Occasionally, there were people in the restaurant and bar who were sober enough to complain, but the situation went unchanged.

Many of our "unwanted" calls to the Old Town Cafe were for winos who had passed out on the toilet. Inevitably, we would get a call on one when everything was overflowing and the odor was shredding the old yellow paint from the walls. We would have to force open a stall door and tweak the wino's ear until he awoke. Sometimes he would be so drunk that we would have to wrestle him out, which was a difficult task when his trousers—sometimes two or three pairs—were bunched around his ankles. Every so often, there would be a drunk who didn't want to leave the stall. In his pickled brain, he had established a homestead and felt he had the right to

114

stay. There were several occasions when there were two or three unwanteds in the cramped space, and when a couple of 200-pound cops were added to the mix, things got real interesting.

While skid row is dangerous any time and any place, I had an intense concern about getting killed in that rest room. I told my partners that if I got shot or stabbed there, I wanted them to drag me out. No way, after everything I had gone through and accomplished in my life, did I want to end up writhing on that slimy rest room floor.

Yes, I was a bit mental about it, but that rest room was really gross.

DISSIN' MY POLICE CAR

My partner, Karen, and I were in a skid row restaurant having a cup of coffee. The restaurant is in an alley that connects two skid row streets, and since the alley is less traveled, it's a popular place for the drinkers to loiter out of sight of roving police cars. We had parked our car across from the restaurant, half on the sidewalk and half into the narrow street, a common practice so that other cars could squeeze past.

We drank our coffee, paid, and stepped out onto the sidewalk. That's when I spotted the wino at the rear of our police car. "What's that guy doing behind our car?" I asked, as I pulled on my coat.

Karen looked. "I think he's . . . damn, that son-of-a-bitch is pissing on the trunk of our car."

I flashed red. Why it made me so mad and why I took it so personal, I have no idea. But I took off like a linebacker across that narrow street, dropping my shoulder into a ramming position as I closed in on the guy who was having the time of his life painting pee-pee designs all over our trunk. So deep in concentration was he that he hadn't a clue as to my approach until I hit the left side of his ribs at about 25 mph—at least it probably felt that fast to him.

The impact launched him off his feet and over to the other side of the car. He landed on his back, but momentum rolled him onto his stomach, causing his piss to fly all over the place, like when a fireman loses control of his hose. He rolled over onto his back again, then again onto his belly (and his hose) and skidded for about three feet.

"You OK?" Karen asked, jogging up to me.

"Yeah," I answered, straddling the moaning man who was now rolled into a fetal position, his hands clutching his groin. "Man, that pissed me off."

Karen made an understanding nod. "I can see that, pard. I can see that."

BODILY EXCRETIONS

PEOPLE WATCHING

"Good one!"

"Almost."

"Oooo, right on."

"Just missed."

"Oh look! He's barefoot."

"Damn! He missed it."

"She hit it. Look. She's shaking her foot."

"Oh man, he stepped right smack in it and doesn't even know it."

"Look! Here comes an uptown woman, business suit and everything. Wham! Right in it. She's looking back at it. Ha ha, she is so disgusted. I give her a score of 9.8."

My partner and I were sitting at the corner of 3rd and Allen, where, 10 minutes earlier, an obese wino pushing a grocery cart had heaved everything he had eaten and drunk over the past two days onto the sidewalk, about 25 feet from our car. Afterwards, he looked over at us for a second, shot us a rotten-toothed smile, then continued on his way, leaving a thick, pink puddle, about 18 inches in diameter.

It was a slow day on the radio, although there was lots of pedestrian traffic on the sidewalk, especially at that corner. To keep ourselves entertained, my partner and I watched to see how many people stepped in the vomit. Some would see it as they approached and quickly maneuver out of the way, while others didn't see it, but luckily missed it by a fraction of an inch. We laughed uproariously when someone stepped in it, but kept walking, oblivious to what they had on their shoe. It was especially hilarious to see their facial expression when they stepped in it, then looked down to see what had made that splatting sound.

"Look, he's making puke prints as he walks on."

"Here come two women. Oooo, they both stepped in it."

117

A HAT FULL OF SUNSHINE

"I really didn't think the guy would do it," says Officer Henderson. "But when I saw that it was happening, I didn't do anything to stop it."

A few minutes earlier, Henderson and his partner, Bardy, were walking their beat on Third Avenue on a day that must have been well over 100 degrees. As they approached the corner, they noticed a guy sitting on the sidewalk propped up against a brick wall. Actually, he was slumped against the wall, deep in a drunken sleep. "He must have been there for quite a while," Henderson remembers, "because the direct sun rays, the heat, and the reflection off the white sidewalk were frying him. The skin on his perspiring face was cracked open, his lips were swollen and split, and his breathing was labored."

"He looks like he's dying," Bardy said, as they stood at the guy's feet looking down at him. "He needs to get out of this sun."

That's when Henderson noticed the cowboy hat lying on the other side of him. "Oh yuck," he gagged. "Look at his hat."

"What?" Bardy asked, stepping over the guy's sprawling legs. Then he saw it, too. "Oh man! That's the grossest thing I have ever seen."

The cowboy's hat was a big white one, lying upside down next to the wall beside the man. The hat was filled—the hole where the man's head normally went—with vomit, right up to the rim. There wasn't a drop on the rim, and there wasn't any on the sidewalk.

"Now, it's possible that the man brought the full hat with him to this resting place," Henderson says. "Of course, he'd have to walk slowly and deliberately so as not to spill, then ever so carefully set it down in the warm sunshine. The natural question, of course, would be why would he do such a thing, but then 'why' is not a question you bother asking on skid row. My other assumption was that someone else upchucked into the hat while its owner slept soundly in the blazing sun. But that inhumanity to one's fellow man was almost too cruel to fathom, even for skid row."

No, the most logical possibility was that the man heaved into it after he drunkenly slid down the wall, probably positioning the opening right under his chin so as not to splatter on anything else. He then carefully set it down next to him and drifted off into a nice little sleep. There was no way the officers would ever know for sure, but what they did know was that it was one ugly sight.

Henderson suddenly had an idea. He says, "My partner and I had never seen this guy before and didn't have anything against him. But nonetheless I had an overwhelming urge to make his day a bad one. Yes, his third-degree burns were going to give him a lot of agony when he awoke and sobered up, but I felt a need to make his day even worse. Perhaps I was motivated by being tired of working skid row every day, or maybe I felt some deep inner anger at how a human can sink to such a low point, or maybe I'm just a damn asshole. Whatever the reason, this is what I did.

"I shook his shoulder. 'Hey, sir.' I says, 'You have to get up now. This isn't a bedroom, and you're frying like bacon.'

"His eyes fluttered open as wide as a quarter is thick, and he smacked his chapped lips. He tried to focus on me, but the sun obviously hurt his eyes too much. He had a serious case of the groggies as he yawned and stretched and gathered his feet to get up.

"'Hey,' I said in my best Good Samaritan voice, 'Don't forget to put on your fine-looking cowboy hat.'

"'Oh,' the guy said, sniffing and coughing. His eyes were still mostly shut as he felt around for his hat. 'Shanks Shoffisher,' he slurred, as he picked it up with both hands. Then, in one surprisingly clean move, he plopped that hat down atop his perspiration-wet head, a move so smooth that he didn't spill one pink drop.

"'Ready for lunch?' I asked, looking up to where Bardy had been standing.

"But he was gone around the corner."

SWEET LOVE

Karen and I were sitting at the corner in our patrol car watching the hordes of street people pass by. It was always interesting to see who had coupled up since we last saw them. It was common to see a gal with three or four different guys in one month; one time I saw a gal hanging all over three different guys within one week. They were usually lovey-dovey until they had a bad drunk together and it turned into a big, nasty fight. Usually what happened was that another guy, who had his eye on the woman for a while and was drinking in the same alleyway, would come to her rescue and whack her boyfriend a couple of times with a trash can lid. Then the new guy, her knight in shining armor, would walk off into the sunset with her (actually, they would stagger off together to the next alley), and love would bloom as they drank until they passed out. They would be together for a couple days, maybe as long as a week, then the scene would repeat itself all over again.

So we were watching the corner when the crowd thinned long enough for us to see a couple on the corner across the street kissing and pawing each other. Both were in their 50s and about as drunk as you can get and still remain standing.

"Hey, isn't that Cindy?" I asked.

Karen chuckled. "Yeah, it is. She was with Flyingcrow last week, that big Indian with one eye."

I laughed and kept watching them tongue kiss as other inebriates staggered around them. "She is sure in love now."

"Man!" Karen said with disgust. "I wouldn't even kiss him with *your* mouth."

"Thank you," I said, still watching them. And I meant it.

After a couple minutes of unbridled passion, Cindy and her new lover stumbled off the curb and began walking toward our corner. She was on his right side, her arm around his waist, his arm locked around her shoulders. They would take a step forward, then stagger a step to the right, take another one forward and stagger one or two

120

BODILY EXCRETIONS

to the left. It didn't help that they were walking so close together that their swaying hips kept knocking each other off balance.

Halfway across the street, and without stopping, they clamped their lips together in another French kiss to beat all French kisses. Karen and I chuckled, and she said something about how bad their breath must be.

Then abruptly, Cindy broke off the kiss, turned her head to the right, and projectile vomited a stream at least 10 feet through the air at what had to be a new world record distance. Amazingly, it barely missed several people who were passing by. Yet only one person yelled something, then scurried on past without looking back. They were still walking toward us as Cindy fired a second pink, chunky stream, her boyfriend's arm still wrapped possessively around her shoulders. He had leaned forward slightly to note Cindy's first heave, then the second, his face void of expression.

Karen and I had seen a lot of vomiting on skid row, probably as much as any emergency room nurse, so we were fairly desensitized to it, though if we had our druthers we would never have to see it again. But as callous as we were, we were not prepared for what happened next.

Cindy's first spew was the record breaker, her second more average, and to her and the boyfriend's credit, both events were executed without either of them missing a step. Then, just as smoothly and without hesitation, Cindy turned back to her boyfriend and they resumed that deep, tongue-dueling kiss.

"Holy shit!" Karen screamed. "Did you see that? They're kissing and she has puke dripping off her chin."

I scooted deep into my seat as my stomach flipped flopped under my vest. All I could say was, "OhmyGodohmyGodohmyGod!"

Karen slapped her hands over her face and cried, "I didn't need to see that; I didn't need to see that."

121

DAMN GRAVITY

"OK, we got it," I told dispatch, slipping the mike back into the dash holder and slumping deeper into my seat.

"Unconscious guy on the third floor. Great. How come they're never unconscious on the ground floor?"

Kathy shook her head and smiled. "We get them, partner. We get them, too. It's just that you don't notice them so much when you don't have to strain your guts carrying their dead weight."

"Whatever," I mumbled as I looked out the passenger's window at the winos sitting against the walls of the Salvation Army building. "Man, we just got out here, and the first call we get isn't to drag one of these guys sitting here at sea level over to the car, but to carry some guy down from the top of a high-rise. Bet you he weighs at least 300 pounds, too."

Kathy signaled for a left and glanced my way. "The call is on the third floor, not the top of a high-rise. Man, you're sure a fun date, today. Somebody shit in your Cheerios this morning?"

"Whatever," I growled. She was right. I was grumpy. But I had worked for several months on skid row without a break, and I needed one badly. I was up to here with puke, and piss, and crap-filled baggy pants. I wanted to work up on Fine Boulevard where a typical call was a fat rich woman distraught over a missing emerald from her poodle's jeweled collar.

"Here we are, pard," Kathy said with far too much cheeriness. "The Richmond Brothers Apartments. Built in 1895, says so right there on the side of the building."

"Whatever," I said, releasing my seat belt. "Hey, it's my turn to carry the feet. I got the head last time." Carrying the feet is lighter than carrying the upper body half.

Kathy laughed and shook her head as she opened the door. "You are such a child sometimes."

Richmond's ancient elevator was broken, of course, so we had to climb three flights of stairs. They should have been condemned too, so rickety were they. Actually, they should have been condemned

122

just due to filth. Everything imaginable and probably a couple of things unimaginable were ground into the old worn wood. The Richmond had been a skid row flophouse since World War II.

"It's Eddie," Kathy announced since she was ahead of me and the first to reach the third floor. The dingy hallway was illuminated by only a single light bulb, probably 25 watts. The smell from years of cooking, puking, peeing, and shitting in the hallway was almost more than I could bear. Eddie was lying in the hall face up, making wet, slobbery snoring sounds. Whoever had called the police hadn't waited around to talk to us.

Kathy twisted his ear and called his name, but he didn't stir an eyebrow. "Man, I can't handle this," I wheezed. "Let's just get him out of here."

"OK," Kathy said. She kneeled behind his head and slid her hands under his arms. "You wanted his feet, so grab 'em and let's move."

I scooped my hands under his ankles and lifted him easily. "At least he isn't 300 pounds. Probably no more than 150."

Kathy strained as she lifted. "Well, I got about 140 pounds on this end."

"Ha ha, you lose this time."

"Just move," she bossed, and I started backing toward the stairs.

From the third floor to the second was a killer. Kathy dropped the guy once and he banged his head on a step. He mumbled something then drifted off again to wineland. We set him on the second landing for a minute to gather our strength, then proceeded to the first floor. I was soooo glad I had the guy's feet because I could feel his increasing weight with every downward step; Kathy must have been dying. We were about eight steps from the first floor when my smugness disappeared with the first warmth that poured over my hands. I knew instantly what it was.

The guy was peeing in his pants, and it was running down his legs and over my hands. And it wasn't just a drizzle; it was a major downpour—at least a quart of that dollar-a-bottle red wine he had consumed earlier.

I screamed and dropped the guy's legs, which made Kathy drop his arms, and once again he banged his head on a step. I was jump-

123

ing around on the stairs, holding my dripping hands out in front of me as if they were covered with piss. Which they were.

"I don't get paid enough for this," I shouted. "I-don't-get-paid-enough-for-this."

Kathy just shook her head and looked at me with a blank expression. "You are so cranky today," she said.

THE EXPERT JUDGE
by Ed Miller
The Rap Sheet, 1978

He was a ranking municipal judge from New York City and considered the foremost expert on skid row flophouses, whatever that means. He claimed to have inspected most flophouses in the nation, authored many articles on them, but I don't know if he ever came up with any answers. He happened into town one day, visited the police station and our municipal judges, and, of course, had to visit one of Portland's typical flophouses.

He assembled an entourage of a couple of our judges, a prosecutor or two, and requested the officers on skid row to meet them at high noon at a flophouse of our selection. I smiled an evil smile because I knew just the place for such an entourage: the old Matin Hotel, smack in the middle of skid row, a place even the rats refused to go.

We used to check the place twice a day to help the manager drive out the worst of the drunks, and every time we went in, we used caution. We had to gulp a lot of fresh air into our lungs, hold our breath, and then charge in and try to do our thing before our lungs collapsed. One also had to be careful of his footing, because the old wooden floor was saturated with human urine, excrement, and vomit and was slick as a shopping mall's ice rink. All of this wasn't as bad as the horde of flies whose constant hum sounded like a far off saw mill.

It was a hot 90 degrees when they arrived, and we forgot to warn them of the stench and heat inside, not to mention the ever-present TB germ. But who needs to warn an expert, anyway? It was about a hundred feet from the front door to the end of the main lobby, where all the winos lay in their own filth. By the time we crossed 40 feet, most of the visitors had departed to cleaner air, leaving only the judge to reach the inner sanctum, though he wasn't looking too well when he got there. "I've seen enough," he said, and we departed much quicker than we had entered.

When we got outside, we were all gasping for air. The judge

125

remarked, "I've been in flophouses in every major city in the U.S., but I've never seen anything to compare to this one."

"But judge," I said. "We haven't even been to the Western Hotel yet. That's a much larger one."

"No thanks," he said, and beat a hasty exit.

A few years later, someone decided the Martin had to go, but I wasn't around when the wrecker arrived. They tell me that the first swipe of the wrecker's ball completely missed the north wall, but the breeze was enough to topple it.

VIEW FROM A WINDOW

One of the first yuppie eating establishments to test the waters in skid row was a place called COCO's, where the owner had leased a corner room on the ground floor of a building that had been the lobby of a flophouse years earlier. I remember being on the second floor only once then, and once was one time too many. The rooms, which people had to pay 50 cents a day for, were 10-by-10-foot spaces separated by walls made of chicken wire. Even to a salty, conservative cop, it was the most inhumane place I had ever seen. A few years later an arson fire killed several of the renters. Years after that it became COCO's

The restaurant owners put in a new floor and windows, added funky lighting, cleaned up the old brick walls, hung a dozen large ferns, and played East Indian music on their stereo system. The suits from the nearby high-rises thought the place quaint and talked about it around their office water coolers, referring to it as a "fabulous little place to do lunch."

Outside the fabulous place, winos continued to stagger by, fall face first on the sidewalk, and sleep against the building's walls. The finely dressed restaurant goers would walk quickly along the filthy sidewalk, looking neither right or left, as if the inebriates weren't there, and then duck quickly into the richly decorated eatery.

The restaurant was at the corner of the building; the windows on the east and south walls looked out onto the mean streets. While most diners chatted away about office politics and ignored the down-and-outers on the sidewalk side of the glass, some occasionally looked out and down their noses at a world they considered to be far beneath them.

I was working by myself one day when I got a call on "a transient disturbing at COCO's." Although I got there only a couple minutes later, I didn't see anything going on outside other than the usual stream of regulars. Inside, I was greeted by the maitre d', who pointed out two women sitting in the small waiting area, both of whom were dressed expensively. They resembled each other, though there

127

was a 30-year difference in their ages. The 25-year-old was using a menu to fan the older one, who was clearly distraught.

"Can I help you ladies?" I asked, sitting down next to them.

"My mother and I have just been exposed to a horrible thing," the younger one said, vigorously fanning her mother.

"It was horrible, Officer," the older one wheezed, her head resting against the wall behind her. "Absolutely ghastly."

"It was the first time anything like this has happened," the maitre d' interjected in a worried voice.

"So, what happened?" I asked.

The younger woman nodded in the direction of one of the tables by a window. "My mother and I were over there eating an appetizer and talking when this horrible man exposed himself to us."

"He what?" I asked, not quite getting how it happened. "Where was he?"

The young woman fanned herself a couple of times. "He was right outside our window when he took out his . . . his thingy."

The old woman leaned forward. "For God's sake, Kathryn," she said impatiently. "Officer, the hobo took out his dick right there on the other side of the glass." Her daughter began fanning her mother again.

"This is a first for COCO's," the maitre d' interjected. "We have never—"

"Then what happened?" I interrupted, sort of enjoying the moment.

"That's not the worst part," the younger woman said, now fanning herself. "Then he . . . relieved himself."

I looked at the older woman. She nodded. "That's right, officer. He took a piss right on the window. His dick was even with our faces and he was no more than a foot away, separated only by that glass— thank God for that glass—and he took a piss right in our faces. And he kept going and going and going. My God he could hold a lot." Her head fell back against the wall and again her daughter resumed the fanning. "It was a horror."

"Lunch is on us, Madam," The maitre d' said. "I promise this will never—"

I interrupted the guy again to get the suspect's description, promising that I would look for him. They said they didn't want to press charges, but just wanted to get safely to their car. So, I walked them to the parking lot and again promised that if I saw the guy I would give him a strong reprimand.

Judging by the description, I thought it might be old Clarence, and sure enough I saw him a block away. He was as drunk as a skunk, and when I asked if he had pissed on COCO's window, he said, "Probably. I've taken lots of pisses today, but I can't remember where I did half of 'em, Officer."

"Well, there were two uptown ladies eating lunch on the other side of COCO's window."

"No shit," he slurred. "But how would I know? I'm so drunk I can hardly see anything."

"Just don't do it again," I said, since I had to say something. Then I turned and began walking back to my car.

"Tell me officer," Clarence called to me. "Was the old bat impressed?"

PART FOUR

CHARACTERS

"I guess one of the things that shocked me
the most when I began working on skid row," says Officer Sanders, now retired from the police department, "was how everyone seemed to support alcoholism there. All the straight people uptown would be quick on the phone to 911 when a wino staggered too far away from the area. 'Officer,' they would say, 'get this horrible-looking man away from the front of our building. He doesn't belong here; he belongs down on skid row.'

"All the social service agencies would ensure that winos, transients, street people, bums, and crippled vets got housed in the skid row area. That's where the low-income housing was, but it was also where the wine flowed.

"There were lots of little stores there that sold bottles of cheap wine for under a buck. It didn't matter how falling-down-drunk a wino was, if he had the 99 cents, he got himself a mickey [half pint of wine]. Most of those stores stayed in business by keeping the winos in a stupor.

"It seemed that only the cops cared about the people on skid row, but in a way, we helped them maintain their life-style, too. We scooped them off the sidewalk and out of the elements when they were passed out, and we got them a place to sleep it off. There were millions of fights in the bars and on the streets, and we were always there to ensure that they didn't kill each other. When they were hurt from a nasty fall, or thumped in a robbery, or hit by a car, we got them an ambulance, or a ride to a skid row medical facility where they got patched up so they could get back to drinking again.

"As long as I worked there, I never got used to seeing all the people lying on the sidewalk. Sometimes when we hit the street first thing in the morning, we would find 25-30 people passed out on the sidewalk, usually the one that borders skid row from the uptown business area. Fine-dressed people would just step over them or around them on their way to their morning business meetings. Many times, I had people in fine clothes yell at me for not cleaning up the eyesore. It never occurred to them that they were part of the reason the drunks were lying there in the first place.

"We got used to seeing people running around without pants—men and women—because after they had shit themselves pretty good several times in a row, they would disgust even themselves and strip off their pants. Of course, there were some who were so out of it that they didn't notice, and they just kept wearing theirs. The smell of the people and the streets was something I still vividly remember.

"We had to be careful not to start thinking that everyone on the row was a falling-down wino. There were people who lived down there because that was all they could afford, or they just liked the social part of it. For example, there was a guy named Rosie who always stood on the same corner every day. He was a black man, monstrously big, who always wore bib overalls. He liked cops and liked helping us keep the streets safe. We would always stop and say good morning to him and ask what had been going on since the day before. He made us realize that there were nice people down there, too.

"We were respected by the street people, the store owners, and the bartenders. The cops rarely got hurt on skid row, other than blowing their backs out from lifting drunks into the paddy wagon. If a new guy in town did punch one of us in the chops, a couple of the big cops would thump him pretty good.

"There were some real characters down there—good, bad, funny, sad, scary, and bizarre. And those were just the cops. The winos were just as extreme."

A DO-IT-YOURSELF JOB

Paul and I got a call to check on sounds of a man moaning coming from a room at the On Broadway, one of many flophouses with classy names. The desk man told us that he didn't want to check on the guy because the tenant was a mental case who had given him problems in the past.

We took the shaky old elevator to the third floor and made our way down the dim, stinky hall to Room 301. Paul put his ear against the door. "Yeah, someone is definitely moaning in there," he said, then rapped sharply on the door. "Hey, you OK in there?"

I raised my eyebrows at him. "If he was OK, he probably wouldn't be moaning, not to mention that we wouldn't be here in the first place."

"Open the door," Paul called, ignoring my dig. A minute passed, but no one answered.

"Use the key," I said. "We got enough probable cause to enter."

Paul inserted the key and nudged the door open. We stood on each side of the door frame and peered in, seeing a small room that was illuminated by a puke-yellow light bulb hanging from the ceiling. There was a ragged mattress on a bed frame, a wooden chair, and lots of empty wine bottles. A naked man lay on the floor at the foot of the bed; there was blood pooled on the threadbare carpet near his groin. He was alone in the place.

"Hey, friend," I said squatting next to the man, who looked to be in his mid-20s. His groin was covered with blood. "What happened here? Who did this to you?"

"Here's the knife," Paul said, pointing at a kitchen knife lying on the floor next to the bed. "It's got blood on the blade." He ordered an ambulance into his portable radio.

"Who stabbed you?" I asked.

The man didn't open his eyes as he muttered, "No . . . one. I cut . . . myself."

Paul and I looked at each other. "What do you mean?" I asked.

"I'm . . . tryin' . . . to circumcise it . . . oh, God . . . it hurts."

133

Paul and I looked at each other as we simultaneously reached for our respective groins. "Oh, man," Paul said, grimacing.

"Oh, man," I said, feeling the man's pain. "Oh, man, that's gotta hurt."

"Yeah . . . it does," the guy moaned.

"Why you doing this?" I asked, remembering what the counter man said about the man being a mental.

"Because . . ." the guy grimaced and took a deep breath. "My parents . . . didn't . . . have it . . . done when I was a . . . baby."

"Makes perfect sense," Paul said seriously, nodding.

"Yes it does," I agreed.

Later, after the ambulance had taken the guy away, Paul turned to me. "I really think you should have applied a tourniquet on the guy."

CHARACTERS

THE JOHN WAYNE IMPERSONATOR

His name was Henry and he was a one-legged full-blooded American Indian. I don't know which tribe he was from, but he was about 25 and had an Indian's characteristically broad face and coal-black hair, which hung down his back in long braids. He wore turquoise jewelry on his fingers and around his neck, which amazingly hadn't been stolen during his years of sleeping on the sidewalk and in doorways. Perhaps he had a never-ending supply and just kept replenishing his losses. I don't remember how he lost his leg—no doubt a work-related accident, and I don't know what happened in his life that brought him to skid row.

I liked Henry. He was personable and never gave us problems. In fact, he even helped me out a couple of times as a witness in assault cases, something that could have gotten him killed on the mean streets of skid row. I didn't like having to pour out his wine when I came upon him taking a chug, but he knew if there were citizens around, especially business owners, I had to do it.

Henry was funny and never failed to crack me up with a one-liner. He also did the best John Wayne impersonation I have ever heard, though it was quite lousy when he was dead drunk. Sober, though, he sounded as good as the real thing and would even include the famous John Wayne walk, which was impressive considering he was doing it on one leg and a single crutch.

"Circle the wagons, pilgrim," he would say out of the corner of his mouth, with that John Wayne tilt of his head. "The Indians are a comin'."

Sometimes he did a variation. "Circle the Indians, pilgrims. The wagons are a comin'." This never failed to send me into fits of laughter, so I had him do it every time I saw him. He loved the attention and laughs, and he always honored my requests.

China Town is part of skid row and is a tourist attraction in the summer. On several occasions, I would be talking to Henry when a

135

family of tourists would ask me which way to, say, Dum Foo's Chinese restaurant. I would give them directions, then ask if they would like to see Henry do an impersonation. They would shoot me a puzzled look, since all they saw before them was a crumpled, one-legged Indian with drunken eyes and filthy clothes. "Come on, Henry," I would say. "Show the folks."

A few seconds later, he would have them laughing uproariously and even applauding.

I haven't talked to Henry for 10 years, but I saw him recently when I was passing through skid row to somewhere else. He's older now, and the hard life is taking its toll.

But I bet he still does a great John Wayne.

CHARACTERS

MMM, MMM GOOD

I don't know about other cities, but in liberal, bleeding-heart Portland, no wino or down-and-outer ever needs to go hungry. There are several handout places—missions, the Salvation Army, food banks—where a person can get three square meals a day. It's hard to find a skinny down-and-outer on the streets, unless the person is so pickled from alcohol that he or she no longer has the sense or the desire to eat well.

Then there are those who follow their own peculiar diet.

"See that guy with his shirt open?" Doug said, pointing toward a tall, thin man walking among a throng of winos across the street. It was a hot summer morning, and my partner and I were sipping coffee in our parked car, watching people walk and stagger by.

I spotted the only man with his shirt open, a skinny fellow wearing a yellow, Hawaiian shirt, its tails flying behind him as he walked against the hot, summer wind. "Yeah. Man, has he got a serious stomach scar, or what?"

Doug chuckled. "That's what I was going to tell you. I got a call on him about six months ago over on 6th. He was rolling around on the sidewalk, moaning and groaning like a woman giving birth. I ordered him an ambulance and asked some of the guys standing around if they knew what was wrong with him. Several of them told me that they think he's got a stomachache from eating a drinking glass."

"A drinking glass?" I asked, watching the scarred man greet a couple of street people and exchange amenities.

Doug nodded. "They said he ordered a soda in Tony's place, drank it down, then commenced to eat the glass like he was eating an apple. He was definitely in a world of hurt, rolling around on the concrete and spitting blood. About a week later, I met the same two ambulance guys on an unrelated call and I asked about the glass eater. They told me that the docs had to operate on him to remove all the shards. They said he downed the whole thing. That's where he got that scar."

We made jokes about it for a few minutes then got interrupted

137

by a call. I had forgotten about the guy until a week later when dispatch sent us to a man down and bleeding, possibly a stabbing victim at Tony's Bar.

As we pulled to the curb, a small crowd that had gathered around the doorway of Tony's parted, revealing a man lying on the concrete. All we could see were his legs, which were extended out onto the sidewalk; his upper half was lying inside the bar.

"All right, who saw what happened?" I said as we nudged our way through the crowd. I looked down at the man on the concrete and immediately recognized him as the glass eater, still wearing the yellow, Hawaiian shirt, unbuttoned as if he were proud of that 15-inch abdominal scar. He was thrashing back and forth as blood poured from the corners of his mouth.

"Me and Lewis did, Officer," slurred a short, red-eyed drunk standing next to a tall, red-eyed, slow-blinking drunk. "It was the God-all damnedest thing I ever did see." The tall man nodded seriously as he listened to his little friend. "He comes in here and orders a damn Pepsi with no ice. A big glass. Drinks it down in one damn swallow."

"One damn swallow, Officer," the tall drunk confirmed. The others in the crowd listened. The skinny man writhed at our feet.

"As I was a saying," the short one continued, shooting his partner a scowl for interrupting, "the sons-of-a-bitch then commences to take a bite out of the glass, like he's bitin' into one of them stale sandwiches they gives out at the mission. Then he takes another."

"And another," the tall drunk added.

"As I was saying," the short one scowled again, "the sons-of-a-bitch eats the whole thing. Even picked up a little piece off the bar and pops it in his mouth, like he'd dropped a crumb or somethin'."

"Ate the whole damn glass," the tall one confirmed.

My partner had been shaking his head. "Maybe we should give him a Windex chaser."

Everyone laughed except for the skinny glass eater in the Hawaiian shirt, who was making some weird noises as he thrashed about on the concrete.

SHAKEN NOT STIRRED

"I had taken someone to the detoxification center early in my graveyard shift," says Officer Johnson. "Then about 2 A.M., dispatch told me to return because I had forgotten to leave a report with the staff. As I pulled up front, I saw a guy sitting against the building's side wall who I recognized as Jerrold, a wino I had taken to detox at least three dozen times. Apparently, he had slept off his last drunk inside and they had just released him.

"Jerrold was a weird little guy, about 45 years old, but he looked 70. He always referred to himself by name. Actually, he called himself by a nickname—Jer-o. He'd say things like, 'Jer-o went to the mission yesterday,' or 'Jer-o needs to get a jug.'

"So he is sitting against the side of the building, his legs spread wide, with a 32-ounce Pepsi cup sitting between them. He has a big rusty nail in his right hand and an industrial-sized can of Lysol in his other. Lysol, you know, is floor cleaner. He apparently had swiped a big can of it inside before they let him out. I asked him what he was doing.

"'Well, Officer, Jer-o uses the nail to poke a hole in the bottom of the can, then he drains some of it into the cup. Jer-o mixes about ten parts water to one part Lysol.'

"'You drink it?' My mouth must have been hanging open a mile.

"'Yes sir,' he says. 'Jer-o drinks it.'

"'Why don't you get real booze?'

"'Jer-o likes the buzz he gets from this,' he says. Then he crunched up his eyebrows. 'Jer-o likes the buzz, but he doesn't like the hangover.'"

OFFICER CROSS

"Cross always had a grump on," says Officer Gary Lane. "He never missed a day being grumpy; he was always mad about something. He worked skid row for a lot of years, never giving any significance to buzz words like, 'sensitivity' and 'politically correct.' He kicked butt on the row and did things the old-fashioned way.

"I worked with him for a while when I was a rookie, and one time we came upon three guys drinking beer on the sidewalk. We pulled to the curb and Cross jumped out of the car cursing, calling the winos assholes and grabbing their bottles and pouring them out on the sidewalk. The winos knew they were doing wrong, but they were on skid row; hey, that's their job. They're supposed to drink and raise hell. Most expect the police to pour out their drinks when they're caught, and they expect to get chewed out; it's all part of the street dance between winos and cops on skid row. Still, Cross came on strong with this big bad attitude and cursed them up and down.

"While he was ripping into them and making a scene, I jotted down their names and date-of-births in my notebook. When we got back in the car, Cross ridiculed me for making the effort to do that—said it was a 'rookie thing' to do. He said I should just pour out the booze and move on.

"Well, I entered their names in the car's computer, and one of them came back with a warrant for bank robbery out of Los Angeles. Cross got really excited, cranked a U-turn in the middle of the street and roared back to the corner where the three winos were. He was convinced that he was going to get a free trip to LA to testify about his big apprehension. He saw himself basking on the beach and checking out all the bikinis.

"We nabbed the guy without a problem and drove him to the station for the detectives to interview. All the way there, Cross was sweet-talking the guy to get him to confess about his bank job; he knew that a confession would seal in his trip. But the wino didn't talk, and Cross got pissed.

"The detectives interviewed him and made a few calls to

California. They found out that the bank robbery wasn't much of a bank robbery at all. Apparently the wino had an account there and tried to get some money, but his account was empty. He stormed out of the bank, walked a block away, then decided to force the issue. So he took the same slip he had used to try to withdraw his money, and wrote, 'Give me some money,' then went back to the same teller and presented it to her. Five minutes later, LAPD had him in the back of their car.

"When Cross heard this, he got really pissed because the bank job was so Mickey Mouse that his LA trip was out the window. 'The fuckin' FBI fucked me out of a fuckin' trip to LA,' he said about a hundred times over the rest of the day. That happened on our Friday, and when we came back Monday, he was still madder than hell about it. All morning he was grumbling about how the FBI 'fucked' him over.

"About noon, we passed by this gay restaurant that had a big window where you can see the cook prepare meals. The cook was dressed like a queen and shot Cross a big smile as we passed. Then he added fuel to the fire by holding up a big cucumber and waving it at us. This sent Cross into a tirade about gays and gay FBI agents.

"About an hour later, we passed by the restaurant again and saw that the cook was trying to get our attention. He had his arms up as if in shock and his mouth was doing this sort of silent scream through the window. Then we saw why.

"There was a wino lying on the sidewalk below the window. He was on his back, his pants were pulled down, and he was pissing straight up, at least three feet. It was like Yellowstone Park's Ol' Faithful. It was shooting about halfway up the height of the window, then splattering back down on the guy's chest.

"The whole time we were wrestling the wino into our backseat, Cross was cursing the fact that the gay guy in the window was alive, the fact the wino was alive, but then he's laughing at the wino at the same time. I don't think I had ever seen Cross laugh before, and it was a little unsettling.

"It was winter and even though it was colder than hell, we had our windows down because the guy smelled so bad. I actually had my head out the window as Cross drove to the detoxification center. Of course this set him off on a tirade about stinking winos, while simultaneously complaining about the 'fuckin' FBI.' He was so pissed by the time we got there that he just hurtled the drunk into the detox check-in area.

"Even the detox people, who are usually super-sensitive and ultra-caring to the disease of alcoholism, were gagging at the guy's stench. They took his blood pressure and other vitals and then, for some reason, removed one of his shoes. It was immediately apparent that his feet had been one of the sources of his odor. His sock was rotted away, which revealed a foot in an advanced stage of gangrene. Cross looked at it, and even he got grossed out. And he was a guy who had seen everything on the row. 'Fuckin' guy stinks, don't he?' he said with his usual sensitivity. Then things got worse.

"When the detox attendant went to put the guy's shoe back on, he knocked off one of his rotted toes. Knocked it clean off and onto the floor. The wino was howling up a storm and Cross was cussing up a storm because he wanted to leave, but now we had to wait for the ambulance.

"When we eventually left the detox center, Cross was beside himself. 'Fuckin' winos,' he said. 'Fuckin' detox liberals. Fuckin' FBI cheatin' me out of a trip. And how about that fag in the window waving that goddamn cucumber at me like that? Shit, this car smells. There's no sense taking it to the garage, 'cause those assholes won't clean it. And there's no sense telling the sergeant about the garage, 'cause all the sergeants are a bunch of fuckin' assholes.'

"Yeah, ol' Cross was perpetually cranky."

CHARACTERS

EASY MONEY

Portland's skid row area was even more of a rockin' and rollin' place back in the roaring '20s, '30s, and '40s. There were red-light districts, honky-tonk saloons, Chinese opium dens, bootlegging establishments, and a series of underground tunnels that led from various establishments down to the Willamette River. Urban legend has it that drunken men were often knocked over the head with a club, then carried through a tunnel to an awaiting ship. Hours later when the drunk awoke, he discovered he was miles out at sea and part of the ship's crew. Another urban legend has it that around the turn of the century a policeman failed to return to the station at the end of his shift. He didn't show up the next day for work, nor the day after. Months later he was found in one of the tunnels; that is, his head was found. His body was never recovered.

Many of the buildings on skid row look the same today as they do in scratchy black-and-white photographs taken in the late 1800s. Many of the old structures are being renovated into trendy restaurants, retail stores, and apartments. If you were to trace the history of any one building, you would find typically that it had been a cattle barn 120 years ago, then a hotel, a warehouse, a dance hall, and then it was empty for 20 years before an innovative entrepreneur bought, restored, and turned it into a modern nightclub.

After World War II, two brothers ran a restaurant in an old skid row building for several years. After one of them died, the survivor held onto the business for a few more years then sold it to two men. They made a few changes and suddenly business took off, with more customers than they could squeeze in. They decided to expand the dining area.

To save money, they hired a couple of winos to tear out a wall. The two drunks worked hard for a couple days, then suddenly quit. One bought a new car, headed to Reno, and was never heard from again. The other stayed, bought some fine clothes and went from bar to bar all over town in a cab. He would have the cabby wait outside while he went in and knocked back two or three of the establishment's finest drinks, then he would take his cab to the next upscale watering hole.

A couple of cops got suspicious and started grilling the man as to how he gained his sudden wealth. "Are you the one doing all these bank jobs?" they asked. The man denied the crimes, of course, but refused to say how he had become so prosperous. The cops wouldn't let it go, though, and stayed on him until the finely dressed wino confessed.

He said that he and his Reno-bound buddy had found money in the wall they had been tearing down at the restaurant. He had no idea how it got there, but he found enough to live like a king.

This stirred the cops' curiosity and they decided to visit the restaurant on their days off. No one knows for sure what they found or what they did there, but not too long after, both of them retired. The police department grew suspicious and there was an investigation, but they couldn't prove anything.

The half-demolished wall was examined and more than $300,000 dollars was found inside of it. There is no account of how much money had already been removed. When investigators traced the history of the building, it was learned that the place had once been owned by notorious gangsters. They had also been successful bootleggers and made so much money they didn't know what to do with it. Apparently, they had never heard of laundering their profits, so they simply hid the money in the wall. It was never clear what happened to them, but for some reason the money was never removed. Then time passed, and it was forgotten. That is, until two happy winos came upon it.

And maybe two cops who suddenly found themselves closer to retirement age than they had thought.

CHARACTERS

U.S.S. MONROE

Her name was Officer Monroe, but she was so fat that everyone called her the U.S.S. Monroe, like a battleship. No one called her that to her face, of course; just behind her back. She was a nice woman with a personality that some would call sweet. But she was just too fat for police work. She stood 5-feet-5, and because she was as round as she was high, her arms couldn't reach around to her handcuff case on the back of her extra-long web belt. Due to the largeness of her curves, her gun on her right side and her radio on the left stood straight out like wings.

She was only with the bureau for few years, spending the last few behind a desk wearing really big civilian clothes. The only time she put on a uniform then was to work the Rose Parade, which is still held each June, an event when virtually every cop has to work mandatory overtime. U.S.S. Monroe was no exception. This was an embarrassment to the other officers because she was always placed in full view on a walking post between the throngs of people and the passing parade. As one officer put it: "No one ever sees U.S.S. Monroe all year long now that she's hidden away in an office. Then when she does put on a uniform, she is seen by millions on the street and on TV."

She worked skid row for a short while, but since it was hard for her to get in and out of a car, she was assigned to drive the drunk wagon along with another officer. She was too weak to lift the drunks, so her partner had to always help her put winos in, then drag them out at the detoxification center. Because she was likable, no one complained about having to do her work for her, though they did laugh at how her gun and radio protruded straight out from her belt. Those who didn't call her U.S.S. Monroe called her The Wings of Detox. As she grew even fatter, she became self-conscious and always wore an oversized yellow rain slicker, even when it wasn't raining.

Since her protruding gun and radio held her raincoat almost straight out, one officer said she looked like Batman in flight.

JOHN LEE'S HATS

John Lee was a grizzled old black man the first time I saw him, and he remained so for the 20 plus years I saw him staggering around skid row. Since we're on the subject, here is something I've never been able to figure out: I have always exercised, taken multiple vitamins and food supplements, and tried to get plenty of sleep, but still I get colds, the flu, and I'm aging in the normal process. But then there are winos like John Lee who drink themselves to oblivion, sleep in doorways, expose themselves to daily sickness and violence, yet they somehow stay robust and strong as they glide smoothly into their 80s. Doesn't seem fair.

Every time I saw John, I thought of the Walt Disney movie where the old black man is singing, "Zippity doo dah, zippity day, my oh my, what a wonderful day." John looked like the actor—even wore overalls and talked with the same heavy Southern drawl, albeit with a sort of growl, probably a result of countless nights sleeping on wet sidewalks.

Toward the end of his life, he walked with the help of a crutch, then with two crutches during his last couple years. But the crutches didn't slow him down, they just provided him with a weapon to swing at people when he was mean drunk.

John liked hats, but probably never actually bought one a day in his life since he preferred to steal them out of cars. I couldn't begin to guess how many car prowl calls I took on skid row where the complainant was perplexed because all that was taken was a baseball hat or a woman's Sunday-go-to-church bonnet. Didn't perplex me, though, because I knew I would later see old John Lee wearing the hat, even when it was a bonnet.

"Hey, John Lee," I'd call out my window. "Where'd you get that hat?"

He would lift his chin, jab his crutch toward me, and growl, "It's your mama's hat. I stole it from your sweet mama."

A few times I would get a call on a man waiting at the corner of such and such, who wanted to point out a wino wearing his hat.

146

John would always hand it over to me without too much fuss, though usually the complainant would change his mind about wanting it back after he saw filthy John close up.

Most of the time John would just curse me up one side and down the other. One time, I was teasing him, tweaking his alcoholic brain, and he squared off and took a wild swing at me. But his lack of glasses made him miss by a mile. My partner and I laughed and we continued on our walking beat, while John cursed up a storm behind us.

The last time I teased him was when my partner and I walked up as he was leaning against a grocery cart full of junk that he had collected for whatever reason. I began teasing him about the woman's pink Easter hat he wore cocked over one eye, and when I glanced over at my partner to see if she was enjoying the show, her eyes suddenly widened at something over my shoulder. I jerked around to see John swinging a large stick at my head.

In the split second it took me to recognize what was going on, my partner lunged past me and grabbed John's arm. I jumped in and we successfully wrestled the weapon away from him. After he was handcuffed, I picked up the stick and discovered, to my chagrin, a large nail protruding from the same end that had been on a straight path toward my face.

I never took John Lee lightly after that. The booze had finally caught up with him and was playing havoc with his brain and his overall health. As the months progressed, it was obvious he was deteriorating, though it didn't slow his acquisition of hats. A year later, I moved on to another job in the bureau and a year after that, I heard he had died.

I have no doubt that he was buried wearing someone else's hat, maybe a fine Easter bonnet.

GOT A LIGHT?

"I'm convinced that most winos smoked," says Officer Waters, who used to work the row. "Don't quote me, since there are no statistics to back that statement, just casual observation on my part. Friends were made on skid row from sharing a package of cigs, but fights erupted frequently over the last one in the pack. The same thing happens in our prisons and, in a way, I think that booze and the cold streets of skid row makes the place a prison to those who end up there.

"I noticed that winos smoked anything they could get their hands on. A half-smoked cigarette tossed from a car window was a blessed find: there were lots of puffs left and it was already lit. It didn't matter where the butt landed—the gutter, water puddle, oil slick, flophouse rest room floor—if there were puffs left and it was lit, it usually brought a joyous smile to the finder.

"One day, we saw Ol' Dean stagger by our car and proceed about half a block before he stopped and leaned against the side of a storefront. He pulled a thick cigarette from his tattered gray jacket and shoved it into his mouth. He was drunker than hell, and he fumbled forever through his pockets for a match book.

"A minute later, we had forgotten about Ol' Dean as we pulled on our coats and gathered our notebooks in preparation to walk the blocks. We got out, talked to a few regulars standing near their car, and began strolling along the sidewalk. By the time we had gotten up to Ol' Dean, he had finally found his matches, which we could see were too wet to light, anyway. Then we noticed something about that big, fat cigarette.

"It was really a tampon.

"Where he got it, who knows, but it was protruding from his mouth like a fat banker's cigar. We watched as Ol' Dean struck a soggy match, then tried to hold it steady at the end of his 'cigarette.' The match wasn't lit, and Ol' Dean's face got crimson as he tried to suck in smoke.

"I felt sorry for the old wretch, so I offered him a light. You know,

148

in the spirit of community policing. I retrieved my lighter and held it to the tampon that was protruding obscenely from Ol' Dean's mouth. My partner kindly cupped his hands around the lighter and tampon to shelter them from the breeze.

"Ol' Dean sucked deeply on that thing and it flamed for a second then settled down just like a lit cigarette. He nodded to us gratefully and with a satisfied look of a man who has everything he could want.

"My partner and I strolled off, knowing that we had touched someone's life, that we had made a difference."

THE APOLOGY

"We had just started our shift," Officer Garten says, "when a robbery call came out that had just happened at a corner market on skid row. Robbery calls down there were usually strong-arm robberies, where one guy would punch another guy in the face and demand his money or bottle. Most of the time, the victim didn't want to press charges but just wanted his bottle back. So we never got too excited about robbery calls there, not as much as the guys did on the east side of town, where robbery calls usually involve a gun in a mini market or in a bank.

"An officer named Roberts was close to the store and said he would take the call, so I decided to cruise the area and look for the suspect. A minute later, Roberts came on the radio and said that it was a strong-arm robbery, that the suspect was a black male, 5 feet 9 inches, and wearing a dark coat. A pretty basic description.

"I decided to check out the Barber Hotel, a flophouse a half block away from the store. Just as I pulled up, a man fitting the description stepped out of the hotel's double doors, so I jumped out of my car and told him to stop. But he ignored me and went into the tavern next door.

"I went right in after him and caught him. When I started to pat him down, he began resisting pretty hard, so I used one of my judo competition throws to toss the guy, which broke a coke bottle he had in his hand when he hit the wooden floor. I got him cuffed, searched him, and found two knives. I took him back to the scene, where he was positively identified as the suspect. That's when I learned that it hadn't been a simple strong-arm robbery, but a knife cutting and a robbery. My suspect had slit the store clerk's throat with a knife.

"I was pissed big time at Roberts for not broadcasting all of the information, info that was critical to my safety and would have changed how I approached the suspect. After I lodged the man into jail, I ran a history check on him through the computer. The asshole was an escapee from Walla Walla prison in Washington, had kidnapped a young girl, raped her several times, then shot her in the head.

CHARACTERS

"Now that I knew this guy was a heavy hitter, I was even more pissed at Roberts for his laid-back approach to the robbery call. He hadn't even said there was a weapon involved. I mentioned it to the sergeant, but Roberts was one of the 'good ol' boys,' so the sergeant just blew me off. I went to Roberts and tried to talk to him but ended up shouting at him when he just shrugged the whole thing off without explanation.

"We didn't talk for a couple years, but then as time passed, we began having coffee together once in a while. We never mentioned the robbery call; both of us acted like it never happened, though there was always a bit of tension in the air.

"About five years after the incident, I invited Roberts to go hunting with me and he accepted. We had been out in the wilderness about a day when he brought up the incident. 'I want to apologize for what happened on that call,' he said to me. I tried to wave him off, but he insisted on apologizing. 'It's bothered me for years, but I've never been able to say anything to you. I'm really sorry. I don't know why I handled it that way.'

"I told him that it was a long time ago, so let's just forget it. A few hours later, Roberts began complaining of not feeling well. Eventually, he got to feeling so bad that he had to cut the hunting trip short.

"He died shortly after he got home."

FRANKENSTEIN

The Willamette River separates the west side of Portland, Oregon, from the east side. Seven bridges, old and new, connect the two banks, including the Burnside Bridge, which arcs over the river, and, when going westbound, drops right into skid row. Because the detoxification center and a few social services are on the east side, winos, homeless, transients, and drug users and sellers traverse the bridge daily.

I was working by myself one day and received a radio call on a guy who had gone berserk in an east side tavern and was now walking toward skid row across the bridge. Dispatch said he had torn up the tavern and had injured several patrons. He was described as 6 feet, 4 inches, 220 pounds, wearing a black jacket and blue jeans. I acknowledged the call and headed toward the bridge.

I had just reached the top of the span when I spotted a guy matching the description walking briskly toward town. I told dispatch that I probably had the guy and to send me a backup car and then I turned on my overhead lights and pulled next to the walkway about 15 feet in front of him. I got out quickly and called to him. "Hold it. I want to talk to you for a second."

He glanced at me, but then kept on walking as if I wasn't important to him. So, I quickly stepped into his path to make myself more significant in his life. "Hold it! I want to talk to you," I ordered.

He stopped and blinked dumbly at me. He was definitely a big one, which gave me the passing thought that being on top of a bridge with a guy this large was not a good thing, especially with eyes as crazy looking as his.

"Are you coming from a tavern over there?" I asked, pointing down the slope of the bridge to a series of taverns and porno shops on the east side. He took a step toward me.

"Hold it! Stop!" I shouted. "Show me some identification."

He stopped about 10 feet away and tilted his head at me. Without being aware of it, I had maneuvered myself so that my back was against the green guardrail, over which and 50 feet below raged

152

the mighty Willamette River. I had another passing thought of being tossed over the rail, then trying to transmit as all my heavy gear dragged me 150 feet under the surface of the water.

"Turn around and put your hands behind your head!"

He raised both arms toward me, then shuffled forward in a move reminiscent of Boris Karloff in the original *Frankenstein*. I pulled my baton, hoping he would find it threatening, but he shuffled forward again, this time stretching his fingers toward me. Behind and below me, the river called my name, but I wasn't answering.

I whipped my baton into his extended fingertips.

He yelped like a kicked dog and jerked both his hands to his chest. His face grimaced as he bent forward, clutching his throbbing fingers with his good hand. One should always seize the moment, I always say, so I jumped him. An instant later, two other officers grabbed him, too. I was so focused on the guy that I hadn't heard them arrive. It took three of us a couple minutes to get him onto his belly and secured with handcuffs.

I was more concerned than I normally would have been with a resist situation because of the river. I can swim OK, but I didn't want to go at that particular moment, especially with 30 pounds of gear on my body and in the middle of January. I told the other officers how the guy hadn't been responding to me.

"You know he's Cuban, don't you?" one of them asked. Skid row had gotten a large influx of Fidel Castro's rejects in the early 1980s.

"You're kidding," I said. "Well, he's the biggest Cuban I've ever seen. Besides, we weren't having a language problem, here. He definitely wanted a piece of me."

The officer rattled off something in Spanish and the big guy climbed to his feet. The officer said something again, and the man walked over to my police car and stood by patiently until I opened the back door. He sat down and smiled sweetly as I slammed the door.

"You know," the officer said with a smirk. "All you got to do is talk nicely to people, and they will give you their cooperation."

"Thanks for the tip," I said sarcastically. Below us, the river gurgled.

SKID ROW
BEAT

WALK, DAMN IT!

O'Rourke was a big cop, big like the way they used to make them. He spent 8 hours a day walking a beat on skid row and the other 16 hours taking care of his cattle ranch. Such was his strength that you wouldn't bat an eye in surprise if you saw him pick up a stray cow and carry it back to the herd. His chest was massive, his arms like tree trunks, and his hands could envelop a fire hydrant.

O'Rourke loved the people on skid row—the winos, the crippled vets, the storekeepers—and they loved him. When he found one of the regulars getting out of line, it was not uncommon for him to whack the wino upside his head, curse him out, then give him a buck for a bottle. He even hired them to work on his place, and they always gave him a good day's work. Uptown jaywalkers and traffic violators often had their hands literally slapped by O'Rourke as he admonished them sternly, but with a twinkle in his eye: "Don't you ever, ever, ever do that again." He would then send them on their way without a ticket. And he never got complaints to internal affairs. He was a big, lovable teddy bear.

The criminal element didn't think so, though. Those stupid enough to break the law on O'Rourke's turf were relentlessly hunted down and arrested. If a skid row outsider—say a hitchhiker with a backpack—hurt one of his people, O'Rourke would arrest the offender with extreme prejudice.

One day he was walking his beat with a partner named Cruise. They were making their rounds to all the usual haunts, including Chief's Tavern. Sally, the bartender, greeted them with a smile as she set two coffees on the counter. O'Rourke and Cruise straddled the stools, exchanged amenities with her, and sipped from their mugs. That's when they noticed the guy at the far end of the bar.

Actually, they heard him before they saw him in the dimly lit dive. He wasn't shouting anything distinctive, just a string of nonsensical gibberish while he rolled his head around as if his neck were too weak to support it. The officers looked at Sally, and she shrugged that it was OK, that he wasn't that bad. But a few minutes later, the

154

guy was getting so loud that he was drowning out the country western music and the drunken rambling of the other patrons. O'Rourke took another sip and raised his eyebrows at Sally.

"He's gettin' to be too much, O'Rourke," she said. "Can you fellas show him the door?"

"Can do, Sally," O'Rourke answered, as he nudged his partner's shoulder. "Let's walk him out."

The two officers walked up behind the man, took hold of his arms, and jerked him backwards off his stool in one swift movement.

"Whatthehell?" The drunk sputtered, rolling his head from right to left and to right again. Sally was busy at the far end of the bar.

"Come on," Cruise said, straining from the guy's weight. "You're walking outta here." The officers struggled for a few steps, both holding him up by his armpits. But the drunk wasn't cooperating.

"Come on, damn it," O'Rourke growled. "Walk. Quit dragging your feet." They rounded the end of the bar, but still the guy wouldn't cooperate. "Walk, I said," O'Rourke bellowed, punctuating his command with a rap of his hard, gnarled knuckles against the guy's bony chest.

"Ooooomph," the drunk grunted, his body vibrating from the blow. But still he wouldn't walk.

O'Rourke, who had the patience of a saint, was getting pissed. "Walk, damn it. Walk," and he bopped the guy's chest with his ham-sized fist. Again the drunk's body vibrated from the impact, and again he went "oooommph" as his head rolled about on his shoulders. But still he wouldn't pick up his feet.

As they neared the front door, and O'Rourke had just thumped the drunk in the chest for a third time, the bartender called out. "Wait a minute, guys." Sally was on the outside of the bar, scurrying up behind them. "The man forgot these. He's a . . . what you call it? Oh yeah, a paraplegic. He's got no use of his legs."

She held out a pair of crutches.

WAKING UP DRUNKS

There are two kinds of passed-out drunks: the dead-to-the-world ones, and those who pretend to be passed out to make themselves look like too much trouble to deal with, in hopes the lazier cops won't bother with them. But I never saw a cop go away just because he thought a wino was asleep. In fact, just the opposite was true. A passed-out drunk was a challenge to wake up because it could be fun to devise creative ways to do it.

I received countless calls on people believed to be dead, only to arrive at the scene and see that it was just Willy or Sammy sleeping off a jug of cheap vino. "I, I . . . think the poor man is dead, Officer," the concerned complainant would say, wringing his hands with concern. "I shook his shoulder, but . . . I think he has passed away. Poor fellow must have just given up hope and—"

"Leave me alone! You mother fucker!" the wino would sputter, swatting at my hand that was twisting his earlobe. Then he would see the concerned straight citizen and spit, "What the fuck you lookin' at, you fat prick? You want to French kiss me?" By then the citizen was scurrying off down the street, wanting no more of skid row.

Twisting the earlobe is still a technique that works more times than not, as does poking a finger into the hollow behind the ear to affect a mild choking sensation. Pinching the trapezius muscles, that band that runs from the neck along the top of the shoulders, works fairly well. Kicking the bottom of the prone wino's foot works on some, while tapping the shinbone with the point of the boot works on others.

If I had gloves on, I would pinch the man's lips shut with one hand and his nostrils with the other. This not only would wake him up, but it would scare the living daylights out of him. Then, just as he awoke, I would snap my hands back, straighten up and stand casually as I came into his focus. He would have no idea why he was gasping for air. It was fun to imagine what kind of dream he must have had in his alcohol-sopped mind just seconds before he awoke. I suppose that was cruel, but it was funny at the time.

CHARACTERS

Ammonia capsules worked like a charm, but amazingly, they didn't work on everyone. They are about an inch and a half long, and when they were broken in half and waved under a guy's nose, he would not only wake up, but he would leap to his feet like a 16-year-old gymnast. He would snot and sneeze for a few minutes, but then have awesomely clear thoughts for the rest of the day.

I recall, however, a few winos who were unaffected by ammonia capsules, even when one was pressed into each nostril. One time, my partner put one in a guy's nose, then stood chatting to me about his weekend as we waited for the capsule to do its thing. A minute later, we looked back down at him and were shocked by the sight of a huge snot bubble growing out of the nostril that didn't contain the capsule. Like something alien, it grew larger and larger, even after we removed the capsule. We radioed for our neighboring beat car to come see it, and in the five minutes it took the two officers to get there, the bubble was as large as a softball.

We eventually loaded the guy into the backseat of our car, and a few minutes later as we dragged him into the detoxification center, the bubble still hadn't burst.

It was quite spectacular.

OFFICER COCKY HAT

He had been on the police department three years and had been working skid row for a year when I met him. He was personable enough in the office, but when he donned his uniform, he suddenly transformed into Officer Cocky Hat. He wore the "bus driver" hat cocked over one eye, like Humphrey Bogart in *Casablanca*, the collar of his jacket flipped up like a character in *Grease*, and he always carried black leather gloves, which he would dramatically tug on before he manhandled a helpless wino. He topped this look off with a giant cigar that he puffed on with an arrogance seen only in big-bellied rich guys driving oversized Cadillacs.

I was a rookie when I worked with him, happy that I had to do it only when my regular training coach called in sick. He spoke little to me, since being new meant that I had nothing of importance to say to him. So, I just trailed in his wake as we strolled along the crowded sidewalks and into packed taverns, where he would stand by the bar until the bartender slipped him a fist full of free cigars.

He was of average height and weight, so he roughed up only those winos who were helplessly drunk and unable to fight back. He would slam a drunk against a wall then slap his face repeatedly until he got the guy's attention. One time I saw him hold both of his leather gloves in one hand and slap a wino across the face with them, like they did in the old days as a challenge to a duel. "Haven't I told you not to drink on the sidewalk?" he shouted in the guy's face, who was too far out of it to resist, let alone duel.

I was just a rookie, but I knew this was wrong. I've trained in the martial arts since 1965, and I have a strong ethical standard as to when force should be used. In those days, however, rookies didn't say anything if they wanted to keep their jobs. It doesn't seem like much of a dilemma now that I'm older and wiser, but it was then when I was new, young, and inexperienced. I told my coach about it and he just nodded that he was aware, but he couldn't say anything either, for fear he wouldn't get back-up from the guy when he needed it.

Officer Cocky Hat continued working skid row after I'd taken a

SKID ROW
CHARACTERS

training transfer to another precinct. A year later, my agency formed Internal Affairs, a unit created to investigate complaints of police misconduct. Three sergeants were assigned to the unit; one was Cocky Hat, who had just been promoted to Sergeant Cocky Hat. Like so many who climb the promotional ladder, he conveniently forgot all the wrongs he had committed on skid row. He quickly became the most aggressive investigator in Internal Affairs, becoming disliked, then hated, and in the process earning a reputation that still follows him today.

159

SKID ROW
BEAT

GOT A DOLLAR?

Begging is an art form on skid row, and those who are masters of the art bring in big dollars during the day from bleeding heart suckers who think they are reserving a place for themselves in Heaven by giving a wino a buck. Of course, the money is always spent on booze and sometimes doughnuts (nutrition is not a priority on the row).

Some street people can get quite aggressive in their demands for cash, which prompted my city to pass an ordinance against aggressive panhandling a few years ago. Nonetheless, it still goes on, and officers get calls daily on scary-looking characters scaring the crap out of straight people who have to pass through skid row.

It can be immensely intimidating to an uptown woman, who is scurrying to one of those "out-of-the-way charming little eateries," when a rag man, with a face that would make a gargoyle look handsome, steps from a doorway into her path and growls, "Gimmee a dollar, you fat, old bitch."

Other beggars put on a face so sad that it would make a bloodhound look happy, as they extend a hand covered with a tattered glove and mumble pathetically, "Please sir, can you spare a nickel? A penny perhaps?" This approach always brings good results, and the beggars often have a fist full of bills by midday.

Some hit up the skid row cops for money, especially those walking a beat. A few of my soft-hearted partners would fork over change, or a couple bucks, others would tell the beggars to get out of their faces or they would knock them on their butts. I learned early on that if I gave in once, the same wino would bug me every time he saw me, sometimes interfering when I was on a call.

One time I was sitting at the usual corner watching the busy sidewalk traffic. I was looking through my wallet for a phone number when a hand rapped on my side window. I turned and looked into the most horrible face God had ever given a human. My guess was that it had started out ugly, and then years of drink and brawling had made it worse. He had the rag man look down, too: clothes torn and tattered and never having seen a washing machine.

CHARACTERS

"Gimmee a dollar, cop," the aberration sputtered, spraying my window with spittle.

"Go away," I said, without lowering the glass.

"Just one dollar, cop. One little dollar for food and a little taste of vino."

He was homely for sure, but he had a convincing sad look. "How long since you've eaten?" I asked.

"Weeks," he said, with a twinkle in his eye, which gave away his real intention. I knew and he knew that the money would go for booze. He was a bullshitter, but he was charming at it.

"One damn dollar, cop. That's all."

I opened my wallet and showed him my twenty. "I haven't got a dollar, only this twenty."

He smiled and pulled his hand out of his coat pocket. "That's OK, cop," he said, showing me a roll of ones, fives, and tens as thick as my forearm. "I can give you change."

THE GYPSY AND
THE CIGARETTES

Her name was Theresa, and she was a young Gypsy woman from one of the many clans that lived and worked on skid row. She was in her early 20s and in possession of a knockout figure and an exotic face that looked more Italian than the stereotypical Gypsy look.

I had about 14 months on the job when I met her. We clicked immediately, though I didn't know anything about Gypsies, such as their codes, customs, and unique way of viewing the world. I just saw a pretty girl who always leaned in my window to flirt and inflate my ego.

On virtually every skid row corner, Gypsy women perched on folding chairs or old broken sofas in front of curtained doorways that led into small rooms. Doors inside the rooms led to living quarters where the Gypsy families lived, a place the outside world never saw. The women who sat outside were mostly in their 40s, heavyset, wearing flowing multicolored skirts, with enough ample cleavage exposed to slow traffic and make even the most stumbling, blind drunk take notice. They sat in front of dusty windows where red, flickering neon letters spelled "PALM READING" or "FORTUNE TELLING." If there had been truth in advertising then, the neon signs would have more accurately read, "PICKPOCKETING" or "WE SCAM YOU OUT OF YOUR WALLET WHILE YOU STARE AT OUR CLEAVAGE AND THINK YOU ARE GOING TO HAVE SEX WITH US." We got a few theft complaints on them, but mostly the victims were married men looking for a little extracurricular activity. Later, when they discovered they were without wallet, or they still had it but it had been emptied and magically replaced in their hip pockets, they quickly fabricated stories to tell their wives. It can be safely assumed that the stories didn't involve skid row Gypsy ladies with tons of cleavage.

When I met Theresa, she in no way resembled the women who perched outside the dilapidated buildings. She probably does today (yes, that's sort of racist and sexist, but I'd bet a paycheck it's true),

162

but back then she was a gorgeous nymph with an arresting aura and a tinkling bell for a laugh.

I smoked off and on for about four years—my last two years in the army and my first two on the police bureau. I smoked Trues, often called "True blues," since they came in a blue package. Not all stores carried them, so they weren't always easy to find. One that did was a nameless, hole-in-the-wall place on a skid row side street. It was in front of this store where I always saw Theresa and would pull up to chat with her for a few minutes.

Early on, she told me that her family owned the store, and when she noticed me tapping out my last True, she flitted into the store and emerged a moment later with a fresh pack. "They're on me," she purred. "My treat for the handsome, young police officer."

That was the beginning of a routine that continued every night for two months. Sometimes Theresa would already have a pack of Trues in her pocket when I pulled to the curb; other times she would tell me to wait for a second, then dash into the store and emerge a moment later with my nightly supply. On a couple of occasions, she returned with a whole carton and would hand them over with a flourish and a dazzling smile. A couple times I told her that I didn't need any cigarettes, since I didn't smoke that much, and my locker at the station was getting full. But she would always run in and bring a pack out, anyway. Sometimes there would even be a candy bar with it. I figured it just made her feel good to give me something.

One day I pulled to the curb when it was raining like a tropical monsoon. I wanted to tell her that I had gotten transferred to another precinct and that I probably wouldn't be seeing her after tonight. She wasn't out front, and she didn't come out of the store, but then it was even too wet for ducks. I decided to run in and say hi and thank her folks for all the cigarettes they had given me over the last two months.

An elderly black man was standing by the cash register with a tabloid newspaper spread out before him on the counter; he gave me a nod. The store was dirty and dingy, lit only by a couple of 60-watt lightbulbs that dangled on old wires from the high ceiling. The only window that looked out onto the street was filmed over from years of neglect, but even if it had been clean, the many plants, most of which were dead, blocked the view, anyway.

Where was the old Gypsy woman I expected to see behind the counter, and where was Theresa? The black man looked too much a part of the place to be an employee. "Is Theresa here?" I asked.

"Don't know no Theresa, Officer."

"What?" I was starting to get a funny feeling about this. "She's that pretty Gypsy girl whose family owns this store."

The old man shook his head vigorously. "No sir. I owns it. I know who you talkin' about, though. You talkin' about that thievin' young woman that came in here all the time. Stole cigarettes, she did. Always had my suspicions, but not 'till day fore yesterday did I catch her. Called the po-lice and they come and took her. Wasn't you," he said, squinting at me. "Some other po-lice. Then a few hours later, two Gypsy mens come here and say they goin' to rough me up 'cause I called the po-lice on their sister. So I called the po-lice again and they comes. Wasn't you that come that time either. It was a real mess, I'm tellin' you. Lots of yellin' and cursin'."

I stood staring stupidly at him. Outside the rain splattered against the dingy windows.

"You goin' to arrest her, too, Officer?"

I coughed. "Uh . . . no . . . I—"

"She was no good, that's for sure. Stealin' me blind every days, she was." He shook his head in disgust.

I never saw Theresa again. The next day I was patrolling at another precinct, far from skid row, and when I returned there 10 years later, all the Gypsies had left.

OFFICER SONNY'S DEATH

Officer Sonny couldn't remember who gave him the nickname "Sonny," or what the circumstances were behind it, other than someone on the row had given it to him about 19 years back when he began working there. He had been walking and cruising the skid row streets so long that he had become a fixture, a well-liked cop whom everyone recognized, especially with his ever-present pipe that protruded comfortably from the corner of his mouth. He was handsome, possessing sort of a man's man ruggedness that didn't threaten other males, though it frequently drew a second look from the ladies. He owned a farm and had that laborious, farm worker walk that so many get from long days of trudging around pastures and barns.

Sonny was one of the nicest officers to work skid row. He treated everyone with respect—criminal, homeless, wino—no matter how low they had sunk. If he arrested a criminal, he made it a pleasant experience, and when he took winos to the detoxification center, he treated them with dignity. But if a criminal or wino got unpleasant, that is, they resisted or tried to escape, Sonny's farmwork-developed muscles would turn the experience into a most unpleasant one.

Several of the skid row women were sweet on Sonny. He was happily married and they all knew it, but it didn't slow them down one bit. Sometimes they would flirt, and sometimes they would just brazenly tell him what they wanted from him. He never yielded, but then skid row women aren't much of a temptation, anyway.

There was one in particular, Sandy, who had been in love with Sonny for a dozen or more years. She gave him birthday and Christmas gifts, and sometimes gifts for no particular reason. She was a wino, but not a fill-her-drawers, vomit-on-her-chest kind of wino. She would get drunk and stumble around, and when the police told her to go back to her room she would. Once in a while we would see her several blocks from her room, so drunk that it would be unsafe to tell her to walk all the way back. Those times we would take her to the detox.

Sonny took her to the detoxification on many occasions, treating

165

her no differently than he did anyone else, even though she would throw herself at him. Many of the skid row officers teased Sonny about Sandy, to which he would just shake his head and giggle. "She's a persistent one, that's for sure," is about all he ever said about her.

Toward the end of his career, Sonny got burnt out on skid row and asked to be transferred to a beat where there were lots of upscale homes, manicured lawns, and BMWs. He was a little out of his element at first, since he had worked in the skids for nearly two decades. But after adjusting, he did a good job there.

One day, about three weeks after Sonny had transferred, Sandy, sober as a judge, walked over to the curb where my partner and I were parked watching the passersby. "Have you guys seen Sonny?" she asked. "I haven't seen him for about three weeks, and I've looked everywhere. Some of these new cops won't even talk to me. I just know something has happened to him." Her eyes were wet, and I detected a sob way back in her throat. I could tell she really loved ol' Sonny, and I was moved by it. It was really special to see gentle love in these crude streets.

"Well," I said, gently touching her hand that was resting on my door. I looked into her sad eyes and spoke softly and with sensitivity. "Maybe no one wanted to tell you, since we all know how much you really cared for him. So I guess I'll be the one to do it—Sonny died."

Like an injured wolf, she threw her head back and wailed a mournful cry that could be heard for blocks. Then, "Oh my Lord! Oh my God (sob) . . . (sob) what happened? Oh, I just can't believe it!"

My partner had scooted down in his seat and was trying hard not to laugh. "You are one sick puppy," he said under his breath.

"Heart," I said. "It was his heart. He suffered a little. Coughed up some blood, but only for an hour or so before his tired old ticker gave it up."

My partner had turned toward his window so Sandy couldn't see how hard he was struggling. "You are an asshole," I heard him say.

"I guess he called out your name once, Sandy," I threw in for added torture.

That did it. She took off in a hard run down the street doing that wolf wail again.

My partner looked over at me and shook his head as if I was the lowest of the low. "I bet they got your picture in the dictionary next to the word asshole."

"Hey," I said pulling out into traffic. "You got to get your laughs where you can down here on the row."

HALLOWEEN

As mentioned throughout this book, there were times in the career of even the most saintly skid row cop when he'd had it up to here with all the filth and human degradation. Likewise, there were times when the most pacifistic wino would get tired of the cops interfering in his life. He would get fed up with having to scrounge all day for enough coins to buy a cheap bottle of wine, then as he settled into his favorite doorway, all cozy and warm under a Salvation Army blanket, a cop would come along and pull the blanket off his head, pry the coveted bottle out of his hand, and pour its contents into the gutter.

Sometimes an observant drinker would spot the approaching cop and try to chug the entire contents of his bottle before the cop got to him. This often resulted in a brief tug-o-war over the bottle, and if the cop was already having a bad day, as was the wino, the situation could escalate into an all-out scuffle.

It was indeed an odd kinship between cops and winos. There would develop a recognition of roles: the cop's role was to keep the horde of winos in line, since no one else knew what to do about them or cared enough to do anything about them at all. The wino's role was to drink himself to oblivion and do it before the cops came, took his wine, and whisked him away to the detox. This bit of street theater went on 24 hours a day, seven days a week.

Officers Dale and Knight were a couple of fun-loving cops who enjoyed working skid row and even liked the winos, treating many of them like old friends. One Halloween they bought face masks—Dale chose a hideous monster mask and Knight a mask of Satan, complete with little horns—and they walked their beat wearing them. They went into Chief's Tavern and were greeted with hoots from the patrons and by name by the bartender.

"Dale and Knight—recognize you anywhere," the heavyset female bartender teased. "Actually, it's an improvement."

"Yeah?" Knight responded. "How would you like the devil to check the date on your liquor license?" Everyone roared and the officers left.

CHARACTERS

They continued walking along the sidewalk and greeted all the passersby as they usually did without the masks. They got lots of laughs and were having great fun with it. The officers turned down a dark side street where few people ventured after nightfall, and since no one was on the sidewalk, they started to pull off their masks.

Then they spotted Otto.

Dale and Knight had taken Otto to the detox at least a hundred times. He had never gotten physical with them but he was always hard to wake up and was confused when he did get his eyes open. Otto was lying along the wet brick wall on a pile of cardboard. A gray blanket covered his skinny form, though he had it tucked neatly under his chin, exposing his worn face to the elements—and to the two officers wearing masks. This was a perfect opportunity, thought Dale and Knight.

"Otto . . . Otto," they called gently, their mask-covered faces just inches from his. "Wake up Otto, wake up."

Otto scrunched up his face without opening his eyes. A hand wormed out from under the blanket and wiped the crud from the corner of his mouth. The officers snickered, then gently, "Otto . . . Otto, look at us. Open your eyes."

Then Knight shouted, "Otto!"

The drunk's eyes popped open, then widened as he stared into the horror of Satan's face. Then his eyes moved down over the police jacket and badge.

"Oh shit!" he moaned, scrunching his face. "They got cops in Hell, too."

DOG-EATIN' SUE

There is no evidence that Dog-Eatin' Sue ever consumed man's best friend, but everyone called him that, anyway. He was actually a Sioux Indian, so it's possible that was his real name and over the years the spelling of "Sue" got transformed. Who knows? His unique name aside, skid row officers remember two things about his personality: he ground his teeth so intensely that it sent everyone running, and he liked to do crazy things as a result of having only one leg.

For a long time, he scooted around the littered sidewalks in a wheelchair, a form of exercise that turned him into an incredibly strong person, especially in his arms. He was a decent person when sober, which was seldom, but when drunk, he was as mean and tough as a junkyard dog. It was common for him to drink himself into a rage, then, at the smallest provocation, hurtle his wheelchair into passing traffic. More than once we would round the corner just as a car smashed into his chair, sending it bouncing down the busy street. One time, an old skid row cop, who had fought Dog-Eatin' Sue a couple dozen times said after such a collision, "Too bad the son-of-a-bitch wasn't sittin' in that chair when that truck knocked it 20 feet into the air."

Not everyone disliked him, though most did. Those who liked him probably did so because they had fun watching him crawl. His "friends" would wait until he was rip roarin' drunk, then bet him a bottle of wine that he couldn't low crawl across Main Street, a four-lane thoroughfare with a 35 mph speed limit, though most drove it much faster. Dog Eatin' Sue always took the bet and, amazingly, made it across every time without being turned into roadkill.

He eventually was fitted with a state-of-art artificial leg. "It was a real good-looking one," one officer remembers. "It looked real and it did all kinds of things: it rotated this way and that way, and bent here and there. I don't know how he got it; it must have been some kind of a special program."

Dog Eatin' Sue liked it because it made a perfect weapon to beat other winos half to death with. When someone crossed him, he

170

would just pull it out of his pant leg and club the crap out of the offending party. Finally, he used it so many times to beat people with that he tore the thing up.

"I hadn't seen him for a couple of days," said one officer. "Then one morning I saw him hopping along a wall on 3rd Avenue dragging that leg behind him. It was all broken to hell: stuffing, wires, and coils hanging out all over the place, and the foot was twisted around and looking funny.

"The guy he beat on must have looked real bad too."

THE BUSINESSMAN

Charley owns a seafood restaurant on skid row, an establishment that has been at the same corner for 40 years, and in the same family for as long. The place is on all the tourist maps, and inside there are pictures on the wall of President Kennedy and movie stars eating the restaurant's famous soup. Charley's father started the business and, like a lot of sons born with a silver spoon in their mouths and handed a successful business, Charley is a card-carrying asshole. However, he is a mover and shaker in town and has some influence with the mayor. He whines a lot about the winos falling down in front of his place and accosting his customers, and while his complaints are legitimate, it's how he complains that makes him such a pain.

When I worked on the row, Charley was continuously on the phone to the captain of the precinct demanding extra patrol and complaining about cops not taking action when he thought they should. He confronted us on the street outside his restaurant and demanded our names and badge numbers when we didn't leap immediately to his unreasonable demands.

One time, he made the five o'clock news when he installed sprinklers under the restaurant's eaves so that he could dowse the inebriates when they leaned against his wall or passed out on his sidewalk. Many humanists were outraged, but the sprinklers stayed in place and actually helped relieve the problem a little.

One day I was cruising by his place and Charley ran out into the street and stopped me. "Officer, arrest that man over there." He was pointing toward a poor wretch sitting against the restaurant's wall knocking back a long pull from a jug. "He's drinking in public, and I want you to arrest him right now."

"Well, there are about 500 other guys drinking out here this morning," I said, just to annoy him a little. "I can't write them all a ticket. Drinking kinda goes with the territory, you know?"

It always amazed me how businesses on skid row, especially new ones, would get so angry at the police because of all the winos staggering around. Hey, the drunks were there first, then all the yuppie businesses located on skid row because the rent and leases were cheaper there than anywhere else downtown. Apparently it never occurred to the businesses that even if we were able to clean up the area, their property taxes and their rent and leases would rise to match the other downtown locations.

Anyway, when I told Charlie that drinking wine goes with the territory, it set him off writing down my name on his little pad, though he had written it down many other times. He said he was going to call my sergeant and (ooooh, my favorite threat) he was going to make a call to the mayor. Well, I ended up writing the wino a citation and taking him to the detoxification center, not because Charley was threatening, but because I thought it might get him off my back, and the backs of other officers for a while.

I forgot about the incident until the next morning when a night officer asked me if I knew a wino named Sanders. I said I had written him a ticket the day before for drinking in public just to placate Charley. "It must have jinxed him," the officer said, "because a big truck took him out at 9th and Silver this morning when he staggered into the intersection. The poor old drunk must have served his six hours in detox, then resumed drinking the moment he got out. About the only thing that wasn't crumpled on him was your citation."

Later that morning, I was cruising by Charley's place when once again he waved me down. "Officer, there is a wino over there, and he is drinking—"

"Yeah, OK," I said. "Hey, remember that guy I cited here yesterday?" I assumed that even hard-hearted Charley would feel bad about what happened. I did. I felt terrible about it, though there wasn't anything that I or anyone else could have done differently.

"Yes, of course I remember," Charley said irritably. "What about it?"

"Well, he was killed last night. Run over by a truck. Still had my citation in his pocket."

Charley kept looking at me as if he expected me to say more, or at

173

least something important. "Whatever," he said with that same irritable tone. "Right now I want you to arrest that guy over there for drinking in public. And take him away from my restaurant. If you don't, I'm going to call your captain and then I'm going to call the mayor."

So much for compassion.

CHARACTERS

WILBUR AND HIS SKIVVIES

Wilbur was one of the top five filthy guys on skid row. He wasn't a bad guy; he was just an absolute walking pigsty. You could have dressed him in the best suit J.C. Penney's has to offer, but he would still come across filthy, unkempt, and with a horrific smell that was right at the top of the list of bad smells.

I took him to the detoxification center at least once a week, usually twice, and that was just me on my shift. He never put up a fuss, because, like a lot of falling-down drunk winos, he didn't find the caged room such a bad place to spend a few hours out of the harsh weather.

No matter how pleasant a wino would be, we still had to search him when we lodged him into the detoxification center. Many guys carried makeshift weapons, something I never blamed them for since the streets could get awfully mean at times. If you have never searched a wino, you are missing out on one of the more unpleasant things to do in police work. I have found everything from old spaghetti to false teeth, which on one occasion didn't even belong to the guy whose pocket I found them in.

I've said that ol' Wilbur was a filthy guy, and he was. He wore clothes that were filthy when they went out of style in the 1950s, and his weathered, boil-splattered skin hadn't been touched with a bar of soap since he was a pup. He had vomit and piss stains on the front of his clothes and wine shit stains as big as a Thanksgiving turkey serving platter on the back of his pants. One time he was even covered with cobwebs, probably from sleeping too long in an old basement somewhere.

But Wilbur was like a lot of guys who, no matter how low they sunk, still had a twinge of dignity. In Wilbur's case, it showed itself in his underwear. Sort of.

One day, as I was searching Wilbur in the check-in area of the detoxification center, I pulled out the rottenest, stinkiest pair of undershorts I have ever laid eyes on. And I've changed some extraordinarily dirty diapers on three kids. You could have dropped those skivvies into a vat of straight bleach and the liquid would have just boiled away without penetrating the horror.

"What is this?" I blurted, as I reflexively dropped them onto the floor. I half expected them to attack my shoes.

"Those are my skivvies," Wilbur slurred.

"Well, I know that. I've just never seen any in this condition before."

Wilbur strained to think through his haze of Mad Dog 20/20 wine. "They're my alternates."

"Your what?"

"Well, one day I wear the ones that I have on now, then the next day I wear those you took out of my pocket." He coughed a raspy TB cough, then added. "You know, Officer, you should never wear a pair of skivvies two days in a row."

I don't remember if I had finished my search or I just didn't want to search any further, but I stopped. "That's fine Wilbur. That's a good way to do it. That's the way I do it. But tell me, do you ever wash them?"

"No," he snorted, as if I had just asked him if he could fly. "What for?"

CHARACTERS

THE GUY IN THE PHONE BOOTH

I had only been a police officer for three months when I got transferred to the downtown precinct and assigned to walk a beat on skid row with a senior training officer named Anderson. He was an old timer and knew everyone on the row, and everyone knew him. They called him Andy.

Rookies in those days were treated like scum: taunted, teased, and given little or no respect. We were called "puppy," and, in fact, we often felt like dogs as we tagged along with the "real" policemen.

One night Andy, a big Polish cop named Ski, and I were walking along a crowded sidewalk. As we strolled, the two senior officers chatted merrily about fishing, and I was supposed to shake the sidewalk sleepers awake and pour out all open bottles. I was trying hard to make an impression with Andy and Ski and look like I knew what I was doing.

As we neared the corner, Ski alerted on someone in a phone booth. "Hey, pup, you need to get that guy's ID and run a check on him for warrants."

The guy he was referring to was a tall, skinny, black man wearing a dress, a filthy white women's coat, and a curly blond wig that cascaded over his shoulders. There was no way I wanted to approach the loony toon, let alone engage him in conversation and ask him to hand me ID that had been riding warmly in his rear pocket. But I was eager to prove myself a real cop, and that I could handle anything they told me to do.

I stepped over to the phone booth, one of those that are mostly windows with a folding door. The guy was chatting loudly with the door open, gesturing with his free hand as if directing an orchestra. Although I had taken a quick glance at his face, enough to see that he had done a terrible job applying his lipstick, he had yet to see me.

I took a deep breath for courage and said, "Excuse me, er, sir. Could I see your—"

A pair of hands shoved me from behind, launching me into the booth and into the guy. It stunned us both for a second, then I heard screams that I thought at first were coming from me; then I realized were coming from my phone booth friend. He was jammed helplessly into the corner, but he was still able to squeal into the telephone receiver. "Eeeeeiiiii! A maaaaaan is in this booth with me, Derek! And he is attaaaaacking me! Help!"

I was pushing and grabbing anything I could use as a handle to get away from him. I must have grabbed his wig because it was suddenly covering his face, frightening him into a long pig-like squeal.

Then Andy and Ski pulled the phone booth door closed, trapping us inside.

"Eeeeeiiiii!" The guy was really squealing now, and swatting at my back in sheer desperation.

"Rape!" he screamed into the receiver, as I yanked at the door. "Call the po-lice, Derek! Call the fucking po-lice!"

"I am the police," I shouted over my shoulder as his hands continued to swat at my back. I don't know if the guy didn't recognize me as a cop since my back was to him, or he was just too distraught to focus. I struggled to open the accordion door, but every time I pulled it inward, it hit my shoe and bounced back closed. I could see Andy and Ski through the glass holding one another as they cackled like school children.

Finally, I got the door open enough for me to escape. I still remember how sweet the air tasted.

A second later, the guy scrambled out of the booth and right into Andy's arms, who cursed and pushed him away.

"Andy," the skinny black guy cried. "Andy, this man tried to . . ." The guy looked at me for the first time through mascara-lined eyes that were large as saucers. "Oh-my-God! He's a po-liceman!" He stepped toward me, his arms spread wide in what was clearly an advancing hugging gesture. "Ooo, you are a young po-liceman, aren't you?"

I quickly back-stepped. "Stop right there, pal." I glanced at Andy and Ski, who were again cackling and wiping tears from their eyes. They were of no help. "OK," I said, trying to get some dignity back. "Let's see some identification."

CHARACTERS

THE OLD BURGLAR
by Ed Miller
The Rap Sheet, 1976

I was driving the street the other day in skid row when I spotted an old-timer hobbling along on a cane who brought a smile to my face. Many of us knew him in his prime as "Spotlight," an old-time burglar who gave up burglarizing after he got caught a couple of times and took two trips up the river to state prison spa.

He was a harmless, silent one who had no friends and spoke to no one except himself. He had a friend once, the guy who convinced him he could be taught the art of crime without being caught. But Spotlight always found himself on the short end of a 60-40 split, and the last time he went to prison, his friend was doing the town with their proceeds.

Years ago when I started working down there, Spotlight would stand on the corner every night waiting for a burglar alarm to go off at the old Montana Assay building, which never failed when the street car went by. At first I thought he was the suspect until it was explained to me who he was and what he was doing there. It turned out he had a hang-up for burglar alarms, a sound that was music to his ears. He always beat the cops to the scene when one went off in his area.

I tried talking to him one night while a noisy alarm was ringing. I waved my hand in front of his face, but got no response because he was in a deep state of hypnosis and would remain so until someone arrived to shut the alarm off. Only then would he return to reality.

Old age and silent alarms destroyed Spotlight's only enjoyment, but if I ever see him on the street on the way to an old-fashioned audible alarm, I will stop and pick him up so he can bask in what will probably be his last bit of heaven and tranquillity.

A FLOPHOUSE DEATH

I got dispatched to a dead body in the room of a flophouse at least once every couple of weeks. One week I went to the same flophouse three times on a "55." Usually, dispatch would put it out like this: "Complainant says there is a bad smell coming from room 108," or, "See the manager about a man not seen leaving his apartment for three weeks."

Once I found a dead guy in a room who had died a month earlier, which meant his Siamese cat had no one to feed it. Being a creative sort of feline, Fluffy dined well, though, eating her master's eyes for her first course, then his tongue, followed by the soft flesh of his neck, and on down his body. By the time we found the guy in his fourth week of demise, there wasn't much left of him that his mother could recognize. Fluffy, however, was one fat cat, and not just a little cranky when she saw that we were taking away her food source.

I got a call to the Luxury Apartment Building, which may have been luxurious when it was built in 1890, but had been a real dive for the last 60 years. Anyway, radio said the manager was worried about a guy he hadn't seen for two days, and he wanted the police to go with him to check out the tenant's room.

I met the manager in the lobby, and we went up to the second floor. "His name is Zeke, and I usually see him in the lobby every day," the manager explained. "It's just not like him to not come downstairs. He's a nice old fella, about 70 years old, I think." He unlocked the door and I followed him in. The room was small with a bed, dresser, sink, and an inset in one of the walls that served as a closet.

Zeke was in bed, deader than a doornail.

He was lying on his back under a sheet and blanket that were tucked into the sides of the mattress and under Zeke's chin, all neat as a pin. I guessed that he had been gone for at least a day, maybe two, but then the medical examiner would have the final word on that. I told radio that I had a 55 and to send the ME and a sergeant, the latter being policy for an unwitnessed death.

I looked around the room to see if there were bottles of medication, which was also procedure. On the dresser top I found only a comb, a checkbook in the top drawer, and nothing in the middle and bottom drawers. There was a toothbrush on the sink, toothpaste, a bar of soap, and nothing else. A gray suit jacket hung in the closet, with pants under the jacket, a white shirt, and an old-fashioned tie, all on the same hanger. The little apartment was neat and clean. I guessed he had been there only a couple days.

"When did the man check in?" I asked.

"About seven years ago, seven and a half, or so."

I looked at the manager. "You said years? He's lived here over seven years? Did he just move into this room?"

The manager was looking sadly at Zeke. "No sir. Been here the whole time. Neat feller, wasn't he?"

The guy must have been a monk, I thought. "Was he a wino? Don't think I've ever seen him before."

"No sir, not Zeke. Think I may have seen him take a drink once or twice in those seven years. Never saw him drunk, though."

I was looking into his checkbook. "Got almost eight thousand in his checking. I don't understand why he lived such a Spartan existence."

"Well, Officer," the manager shrugged. "That's just the way the man was."

I pulled down the covers from Zeke's bare chest. "Uh oh," I said. "This doesn't look good. Looks like Zeke's been shot."

The manager stepped closer and saw what I was looking at. There was a small hole right over Zeke's heart. "Looks like a .22 round," I said, reaching for my radio. I asked dispatch to send a homicide team and to update the sergeant.

The ME got there first, a white-haired veteran who must have been in his early 60s. He had a solemn face that I assumed went with his job. "What do you have?" he asked, stepping up to the bed.

"Looks like a small handgun wound, maybe a .22. Just a drop of blood."

The ME nodded and then started poking around on old Zeke's frame. "Uh huh," he mumbled as he looked at Zeke's back, then poked his gloved finger into the wound. "Uh huh . . . uh huh."

181

After a few minutes, the old ME straightened and pulled off his gloves. "It's a natural."

"Natural causes?" I said amazed. "What about the hole in his chest? That's not a bullet hole?" I'd seen a few in my career.

The ME shook his white hair. "Nope. Heart attack. Did it so hard he blew an aorta."

"That can make a hole in a guy's chest?"

The ME nodded again. "Doesn't happen often, but it does happen."

"Damn," I said, looking down at Zeke. I looked again at the bare apartment that the man had called home for over seven years. I told the ME how long the man had been living in it.

"Not much in the way of pleasantries," he said, giving the room a quick glance.

I looked around again. First the revelation about the room, then the revelation about the heart attack. "Man. Some people are just a lot more interesting in death than when they were alive."

The ME, who had been to thousands of death scenes, nodded. "Yup."

CHARACTERS

OLD MARY F.
by Ed Miller
The Rap Sheet, 1975

We got a postcard the other day from an old-time skid row regular. She announced that she was on the way back to Portland and had gotten married again. At last count, Mary had been married 225 times, but never bothered changing her last name because when the groom wakes up sober the next morning and sees what he got into, he escapes down the fire escape.

Whenever she used to come in, I would send her up the stairs to the Youth Division, just to get rid of her, but so far she has never been sober enough to navigate the stairs. She fears stairways, anyway, because, as she says, it isn't so bad going up, it's coming down headfirst that hurts so much.

Mary really isn't that old, but she still insists she witnessed the massacre of the 7th Cavalry under General Custer. She claims she was hiding in some brush and was close enough to Custer to hear his last words, which were: "How come all these guys are so mad at us? Last night they were all dancing."

THE BOTTLE IS THE DEADLIEST WEAPON
by Ed Miller
The Rap Sheet, 1976

Now that you know all about skid row, let's turn the page and look around the corner. It's still there, but the skid row of old is being driven out. Most of the old regular winos are dead now, and the few remaining are subject to burial at any given time. How they survive as long as they do is something of a medical mystery. But for every older one who meets his Maker, there is a younger one to take his place.

Skid row today is divided between two entirely different elements: the alcoholic derelicts on one side who drink up the taxpayers' money, and the citizens and merchants on the other side who have to pay for their way of life. It's almost strange how the two have learned to live with each other.

No one knows what it costs to keep a derelict alive, and some wonder why we even try. Take the case of Robert S., a battered wino who had more stitches in his head than all the baseballs in America. Robert is seldom in a vertical position, and every day he is taken to either the detoxification center, jail, or the county hospital, all of whom whisk him out as soon as possible, considering him a hopeless case.

Then there is the do-gooder who walks up and asks, "Why don't you cops do something with that guy?" That calls for a zonk on the head, but, of course, we can't do that. But I swear, the next one who asks me that is going to find a whole wagonload of Roberts in his front yard.

Skid row is a high-crime area, but how high is it? Every time Robert falls down and splits his head, he claims he was slugged and robbed, sometimes twice a day. If that were the case, he would have to be the richest wino in the land. With a total income of $68 a month from welfare, all of which goes for booze, it would be slim pickings for any jackrollers; on the other hand, exposed nickels and dimes can get you killed on the row.

Then there is the inventive wino who discovered he could go to the welfare office, claim he had been robbed, and receive another stipend. There is one stipulation: he has to make out a police report first. I bit on that one once and suddenly found myself confronted with two of his pals who also wanted to make police reports. Then three times over the next three days, winos were found down with split heads, all of whom were sent to the hospital. In each case, they claimed they had been slugged and robbed. Witnesses gave another story: the "victims" were staggering down the street, fell, and received injuries. One wino said he lost $400, another $140, but the fact is that each one was on welfare just like Robert. That was nipped fast, and I hope welfare did the same because those are our dollars they are giving away.

But there are other winos, lovable ones who hurt no one but themselves. There is young John R., a likable kid who is really hurting in the morning when he is on the juice. He knows where to find me when I come to work and is there waiting for a loan. I try to deny him a buck because I know it's another nail in his coffin, but what can you do? He hangs on my gun belt until I give in, since it looks ridiculous for a cop to be dragging a wino down the street. Besides, it could almost be considered police brutality not to cure John's shakes by giving him a buck for his first jug.

Then there is old Ralph S., who takes pride in being the smelliest and scroungiest wino in the United States. He is a solitary soul who wants to be friendly, but no one will get within 20 feet of him. I watched with interest one morning while one of our officers tried to do something cops have been trying to do for 20 years—give him a bath. He had to hogtie Ralph and haul him to the Cleanup Center where a miracle was performed. Ralph was screaming about his civil rights all the way, but he emerged freshly scrubbed with a change of clean clothes. The officer felt proud of his accomplishment but was off the next two days, and when he came back, I didn't have the heart to tell him Ralph had crapped his new britches two days in a row.

And how about Briarpatch, skid row's technical advisor? He is in a class all by himself. He is completely indestructible, and I predict he will live to be 125 years old, especially after observing the accident he had the other day. He was sitting on his usual perch, atop the doors of the sidewalk elevator at 9th and Bibbs, enjoying a sunny "happy hour." The store proprietor took the elevator down to the basement for supplies and was soon joined by Briarpatch. Only he didn't take the elevator—he went down the hard way, head first. He was whisked away by ambulance but was back in an hour with a Band-Aid on his head. The only damage was to the concrete floor in the basement, which had a piece chipped away by Patch's head. We have ordered a crash helmet for him as we don't want to lose him. He gives the neighborhood atmosphere.

Young Gus L. is a walking basket case. Subject to seizures and with a plate in his head, he has been another expensive wino to the taxpayers. He knows he is a candidate for a slab at the morgue, but he couldn't care less. He lives only for the jug and one more day of oblivion. So desperate is he for a drink, there are times he will take a drink of water to squelch the flames within.

Who was Charles G. and where did he come from? He was a newcomer and a likable guy who never drew a sober breath during his short life on the row. He, too, had to be removed from the streets every day. He always posed a problem since he was on crutches and no agency wanted him. It's ironic that Charles recently posed for a picture with all of the skid row cops. Shortly after, he disappeared, then a while later, his decomposed body was found floating in the river.

I'm sure Charles knew better days, like Vietnam, where he was decorated with a Purple Heart. Perhaps he was a victim of war, one of the many who survived only to die in the gutter by another deadly weapon, the bottle. They say Charles faced amputation of his leg, which prompted him to end it all.

Perhaps it's time for the state's legislators to go back to the drawing board. Their humane drunk law gave the alcoholics the right to stay drunk permanently, and often there is no place to take them to dry out. We can't take a drunk to jail for protective custody, and the detoxification center won't take them if they can't walk.

CHARACTERS

"Send them to the hospital," some say. Well, if you want to see busy nurses and doctors lose their cool, do it.

"Leave them lying on the sidewalk," others say, but they don't have to listen to citizens' complaints like we do. The winos have been there a hundred years, and they will be there tomorrow. As usual, the police are caught in the middle—damned if we do, damned if we don't. Those of us working down there are mere sweepers of human flotsam.

ABOUT THE AUTHOR

Loren Christensen's experience in law enforcement began in 1967 when he served in the army as a military policeman in the United States and in Vietnam. He joined the Portland, Oregon, Police Bureau in 1972 and retired 25 years later in 1997. During those years, he specialized in street gangs, defensive tactics, dignitary protection, and patrolling the bizarre streets of skid row.

He now writes full time and teaches martial arts. Check him out on his web site at:

http://www.aracnet.com/~lwc123/